Live A Life

That Is Pleasing To

GOD

And Receive His
Best

ODELL YOUNG, JR.

Live A Life

That Is Pleasing To

GOD

And Receive His
Best

ODELL YOUNG, JR.

SER**V**ANTE
PUBLISHERS

Palmetto, GA • 30268

ISBN-13: 978-0615836959
ISBN-10: 061583695X

Printed in the United States of America

For Speaking Engagements, Book Orders, or additional information, contact Odell Young, Jr.:

Email: odell.youngjr@gmail.com
Phone: 404-319-0913
Mail: P.O. Box 801
           Palmetto, GA. 30268

Dedication

Everything in the universe is made of matter and the building block of matter is the atom. The Spirit of God fills, occupies, and controls every atom in the universe and He commands every atom whenever He desires. God can also influence the thoughts and actions of all people. In writing this book, I asked God to influence my thoughts in such a way that I may put in writing the things the children of God should do to live a life that is pleasing to Him. Through the following pages, you will see a common thread in the things that the children of God should do to live a life that is pleasing to Him.

With this in mind, I give God the credit for the full content of the words that are contained in this book. I even received the title from God, who is always available when I call on Him. He is my senior partner in my relationship to Him and I am the subordinate partner. The Bible tells me I cannot do anything without Him. Believe me; I do not even try because I believe Scripture from Genesis to Revelation. I dedicate this book to the Father, the Son, and the Holy Spirit.

In Memoriam

I dedicate this book to the memory of my mother, Mrs. Lillie M. Young, whom I loved very much. She unknowingly planted a seed in my mind when I was 22 years old to be a minister. God germinated the same seed years later on October 20, 2007, when He called me into the ministry to be an ambassador for Jesus Christ.

Contents

CHAPTER ONE
OUR RELATIONSHIP WITH GOD
3

CHAPTER TWO
GOD WANTS TO CHANGE YOU
9

CHAPTER THREE
DEVELOPING YOUR FAITH
13

Chapter Eight
Choose Life
45

Chapter Nine
Fear God (And Nothing Else)
51

Chapter Ten
Confessing Jesus
55

Chapter Eleven
God Owns Everything
61

Chapter Twelve
He Gives Us Power Over Sin
67

CHAPTER TWENTY-TWO
GOD WANTS TO PROVIDE FOR YOU
131

CHAPTER TWENTY-THREE
WE ARE THE RIGHTEOUSNESS OF GOD
139

CHAPTER TWENTY-FOUR
GOD'S SERVANTS WHO DISPLEASED HIM
147

Acknowledgements

I truly believe that there is a motivational factor behind a great author. The inspiration behind my writing is the anointing of the Holy Spirit. He infiltrates the reservoir of my thoughts with His own thoughts to add substance to my writing. From my years of studying Scripture, I am always supplied spiritual thoughts to write and speak about.

Scripture teaches us that if we abide in Jesus and He abides in us, we can produce much fruit. For I know that God constantly gives me the power to write and speak on the things of God. I am never void of things to say about the word of God.

I must acknowledge the time and effort of my mentor, Michael Coley, who has invested countless hours sharing with me the secret things of God. Michael is an apostle of God in Christ. I also acknowledge his lovely wife Venetta, who understands the high calling God has placed on Michael's life.

I also thank my adorable wife Delores for her support and understanding of the high calling that God has also placed on my life. She has also helped in the typing and editing of this manuscript. Next, I give thanks to my three children Angela, DeAnn and Kevin for their patience in giving me the privacy necessary to spend countless hours in solitude with God in studying and meditating on His word.

I believe God prepared my family in my writing this book. Because many hours were invested in bringing all the material together that required total concentration and my undivided attention. This book would not be possible without the assistance of the Holy Spirit, because many times in writing this book God would place a thought in my mind that would give me the answer to something that I needed to say that would agree with Scripture.

Introduction

Jesus Christ's life on earth was an example of the life that God wants His children to live. In every aspect of His life, He demonstrated the lifestyle that we must follow to be pleasing to God. He also defined what love is all about in His interaction with people. Jesus had compassion for all people.

Throughout the pages of this book, I will attempt to lay out for you the reader, what God expects of you and your actions toward other people. God had a plan for you long before you were even in your mother's womb. Scripture teaches us in *Jeremiah 1:5, "Before I formed you in your mother's womb I knew you."* Your entire life centers on God's plan for you. In fact, God's plan is your life. The only way for you to live the life God intended for you to live is to seek Him and discover the plan He has for you. God's plan for you includes your assignment and future and the hope He has for you. The lesson, found in *Jeremiah 29:11 (NIV),* is *"For I know the plan I have for you, says the Lord, to prosper you and not harm you, to give you a future and a hope."* Once you get to know God, you will discover that He has your life already laid out for you.

Chapter One

Our Relationship With God

"That they all may be one, as You, Father, are in Me, and I in You, that they also may be one in Us, that the world may believe that You sent Me."
John 17:21

"I in them, and You in Me; that they may be made perfect in one, and that the world know that You have sent Me, and have loved them as You have loved Me."
John 17:23

GET TO KNOW YOUR HEAVENLY FATHER

Most people know about God, but a much smaller number of people really know Him. People who diligently seek Him to know Him will eventually experience a true relationship with the Father. I do believe that people who really want to know the truth and search the word of God with a pure heart will find God.

Moreover, He will begin to reveal more of Himself once he sees that you have made a commitment to know Him. Notice how King David instructed His son Solomon on how to seek God. *"As for you, my son Solomon, know the God of your father, and serve Him with a loyal heart and a willing mind; for the Lord searches all hearts and understands all the intent of the thoughts. If you seek Him, He will be found by You; but if you forsake Him, He will cast you off forever."* **1 Chronicles 28:9**

The Holy Spirit will also play a part in your knowledge of God. He will lead into all truths of the Father. For the Holy Spirit is the messenger of God and He only gives you what He has heard from the Father. As your relationship develops with God, He will begin to speak to you in one or more ways. God speaks to me in my thoughts. He speaks to me through His word. Sometimes God will speak to you through someone else. God wants a personal relationship with all of His children. Moreover, this relationship is demonstrated through His relationship with His son Jesus Christ. To know Jesus is to know God for they both are the same. Jesus is God in the flesh. And, Jesus is God in the Spirit. When Jesus walked on the earth and talked with people, they did not know that they were actually talking to God. They actually heard the voice of God and did not know it. For Jesus and God cannot be separated for they are both One and the same. Scripture teaches us that Jesus has always been God from the beginning: *"In the beginning was the Word and the Word was with God and the Word was God." **John 1:1*** *"And the Word became flesh and dwelt among us, and we beheld His glory, the glory as of the only begotten of the Father, full of grace and truth." **v:14***

This act of God presenting Himself as Jesus in the flesh is one of the many miracles that God performed for the world to see and for the world to know.

ALWAYS LIFT UP JESUS

When we understand that God has given all power and authority to Jesus, it is time to lift up the name of Jesus everywhere. Scripture teaches us in **Matthew 28:18**: *"And Jesus came and spoke to them saying, "All authority has been given to Me in heaven and earth."* We should do everything on earth in the name of Jesus because He is our Lord. There is power in the name of Jesus. Scripture tells us that Jesus was with God in the beginning. He created the earth and He made everything in it. Whenever we ask God for anything, we should ask in the name of Jesus. He is our High Priest who has been tempted in every way, but has never sinned. He is without any blemish or spot for He is perfect in every way. Because He was offered as a sacrifice for all, we were "saved" and able to escape eternal damnation. When you were baptized, were you not baptized into His death? When we were baptized, we died in Christ, sin has no place in us any longer for we live and walk in the newness of life through Jesus our Lord. Jesus is everything to the believer and we should always lift Him up, because He paid the full price for our salvation. Jesus is at the right hand of the throne of God today interceding on behalf of the children of God. He is our advocate who is pleading to God for us. Scripture tells us that any man who acknowledges Jesus before other men, He would confess that man's name before the Father. For Jesus is our life and our life belongs to Him.

In **Hebrews 12:2** it says *"Looking unto Jesus, the author and finisher of our faith, who for the joy that was set before Him enduring the cross, despising the shame, and has sat down at the right hand of the throne of God."* Jesus said, *"If I be lifted up I will draw all men unto Me." **John 12:32***

We must lift up the name of Jesus whenever there is the opportunity. It is the will of our Father that we always lift up the name of Jesus Christ our Savior.

SEEK HIM FOR INSTRUCTIONS

Scripture teaches in **Proverbs 12:1** *"Whoever loves instructions loves knowledge."*

I do believe that God is always giving instructions to His children who are listening and paying close attention. God's word is always the instructions for His children to live by. However, we can also petition Him in prayer for specific instructions and He will give us our request. You must pay very close attention when you are waiting for God to give you instructions because the answer could come to you at any time and any place. Often the answer to your request may not seem practical to you at first. You must remember that God's ways are not our ways, so do not question His instructions when they come. Just move on in faith and obey the instructions from Him. Do you remember the woman with the issue of blood who had suffered with this ailment for twelve years? The Bible does not state that she had received the instructions from God. However, God was the one who saw to it that she received the instructions to touch the hem of Jesus' robe. She received an instant healing from God by following instructions. In *GENESIS 4*, God gave clear instructions to Cain and his brother Abel on how to present an offering to Him. God had instructed the two brothers to give the first and the best fruit of their harvest. Cain gave his offering but it was not his best or his first so God did not respect Cain's offering. Cain was angry. Abel gave the first and best of the fruit of his harvest; and God was pleased with his offering. Cain later killed his brother Abel because God accepted the offering from Abel, and rejected his offering.

It pleases God to give instructions to His children who ask Him. When we ask God for instructions about something that we want, it demonstrates our dependency on God. If we do not ask God for help and we try to get the answer our own way, it shows that we are not dependent on God for everything.

The widow in Sodom who lived alone with her son had only one meal left for herself and her son. Elijah approached her at her gate. He asked her for food and drink. She told him that she only had enough food for herself and her son; and after that, they would starve to death. Elijah gave the woman instructions to make a meal for him first and they would have enough food to live on for many months. The woman followed the instructions given by Elijah and she had enough flour to last many days until the Lord sent rain on the earth.

We can call on God today to give us instructions and He will do the same for us because God is not a respecter of person. He will give His children what they ask if they are living a life that is pleasing to Him.

Chapter Two

God Wants To Change You

"Brethren, I do not count myself to have apprehended; but one thing I do, forgetting those things which are behind and reaching forward to those things which are ahead." **Philippians 3:13**

"Therefore we were buried with Him through baptism into death, that just as Christ was raised from the dead by the glory of the Father, even so we also should walk in newness of life." **Romans 6:4**

PUT OFF YOUR OLD CONDUCT

Once saved, you are a member of the family of God. God will train you and teach you His ways, which are different from the ways of the world. God wants you to have a different character than what you had in the world. A new character is what God wants for you, one that is pleasing to Him. Scripture teaches us in *2 Corinthians 5:17* "Therefore, if anyone is in Christ he is a new creation; old things have become new," You will no longer desire to go places where you once went or do things that you once did. You will not desire to follow the same crowd you once followed.

Your old friends that are unbelievers will not understand the new you. They will notice a difference in your conduct and behavior. You will also begin to walk in the Spirit and not in the flesh. The Spirit of God will begin to lead and direct your life in the ways of God. The Holy Spirit will also act as a guide to lead you into all the righteousness of God. Jesus, who now is abiding in you, will be your new life. He will be a senior partner to you and a friend. As you live this new life, you are now a representative for God through Jesus Christ.

FORGET YOUR PAST

Scripture tells us it is wise to forget those things that are behind us and reach for those things that are ahead of us. I do not remember Jesus telling His disciples to consider those things that are in the past. The past is only history, to be considered only as history and nothing else.

We can certainly learn from our past, but we should never dwell on the past. We should always be reaching for the things that are before us and the things that God wants to do in our lives. Never try to relive the past, for we can do nothing about the past. God has a plan for each of His children and it is all about the future and not about the past. We should always be reaching for those things that are ahead and press toward the goal for the prize of the High call of God through Jesus Christ our Lord. God has a plan for every one of His children according to *Jeremiah 29:11, "For I know the plans I have for you, says the Lord, thoughts of peace and not of evil, to give you a future and a hope."* It is the will of God that you forget your past, and focus on the new life that He has for you.

PUT OTHERS FIRST

It is always the righteousness of God to consider the needs of others before ourselves. For this is pleasing to God when we put others before ourselves. Especially the needs of others who cannot help themselves. In observing the life of Jesus as He walked among others, I do not ever recall Him discussing His own needs. He was always concerned about the needs of others. Moreover, I am sure that one of the reasons God placed Jesus among people was to demonstrate how we should care for one another. Our first responsibility is our own family and relatives and next for those who are close to us. When we think about the special love God has for His own children, we should extend the same love to others. This is pleasing to God because we are acting out the second commandment that God gave to Moses—to love our neighbor as we

11

love ourselves. We do not have to look very far today to find someone who needs love or just a kind word. God demonstrated an act of love by sending His Son into the world to die in order to save men from their sins. We were headed to eternal damnation because of our sin debt that someone had to pay. God saw to it that we would not have to pay this debt and consequently all of God's children escaped the penalty of death and hell. God made it so simple for man to receive salvation. The only requirement to receive the gift of salvation is for anyone to confess with his mouth that Jesus is Lord and believe in his heart that God raised Jesus from the dead. This teaching can be found in **Romans 10:9.**

Chapter Three

Developing Your Faith

"Looking unto Jesus, the author and finisher of our faith, who for the joy that was set before Him endured the cross, despising the shame, and has sat down at the right hand of the throne of God." **Hebrews 12:2**

"But without faith it is impossible to please Him, for he who comes to God must believe that He is, and that He is a rewarder to those who diligently seek Him." **Hebrews 11:6**

COMMIT YOUR LIFE TO HIM

"Therefore know that the Lord your God, He is God, the faithful God who keeps covenant and mercy for a thousand generations with those who love Him and keep His commandments." **Deuteronomy 7:9**

God desires a close relationship with all of His children. He does not want a relationship that is sometimes hot and other times cold. He wants a full committed relationship, which is needed to train each of His children. How can God train a child who is lukewarm to His way of living? A lukewarm person will not be consistent and so he is not teachable. God delights in a believer who is diligent in his pursuit of the things of God. Scripture teaches us that God will reward the diligent, and the lukewarm He will cast away. See **Revelation 3:15**, *"I know your works, that you are neither cold nor hot. I could wish you were cold or hot." So then, because you are lukewarm, and neither cold nor hot, "I will vomit you out of My mouth."*

God is disclosing the type of relationship that He wants with His children. He is looking for a believer that is diligent and fully committed to Him. He is not interested in a believer that is not committed or is lukewarm. How can God give you His best if you are not diligent or committed to Him?

Why is God concerned about every aspect of your life? He is a loving Father who wants the best for you in every way. He also wants your best and your best is your commitment to Him and His word. He wants you to bring all of your concerns to Him and not try to operate in your own strength and go your own way. For God knows that when one of His children does this He is destined to fail. It is called prodigal living that will end up being a waste of effort and time.

There is an example of a situation like this in *Luke 15:11-20:*

A certain man had two sons. And the younger son said to his father give me the portion of goods that falls to me, so he divided to them his livelihood. Not many days after, the younger son gathered all together, journeyed to a far country, and there he wasted his possessions with prodigal living. But when he had spent all, there arose a famine in that land, and he began to be in want. Then he went and joined himself to a citizen of that country, and he sent him to his fields to feed the swine. And he would gladly have filled his stomach with the pods that the swine ate, and no one gave him anything.

This young man later came to his senses and decided to go home to his father who received him with open arms.

God wants you to depend on Him and not stray from Him like the prodigal son. God knows what is best for each of His children. In addition, He wants to give each of His children the best He has to offer.

Wait On God

God will require all of His children to wait on Him to demonstrate patience, which is one of the fruits of the Spirit. For this is part of the training of God. I have noticed that God also required many of the characters of the Bible to wait. Moses, Abraham, Joseph and David just to name a few, were all required to wait on God's timing. It is not human nature to want to wait. God understands this, but He still insists that we wait on His timing and not on our timing. I do believe that one of the ways that God uses to test our love for Him is to make us wait when we have asked Him for a blessing in our life. If we truly love God above anything else, we will demonstrate patience and wait on Him. If our love for God is lukewarm, I believe that we will not wait very long on Him. This is why God said lukewarm children could not serve Him.

Scripture teaches us that God is good to those who wait on Him. It is always best to wait on God who always has our best interest at heart. Waiting on God demonstrates trust in Him and His word. The Holy Spirit will assist us in waiting on God for He is our Comforter and Helper. Remember, there is always a reward for waiting on Him. There are always consequences when we decide to go ahead of God and not wait on Him. This happened to the Israelites in the wilderness. God kept Moses on Mount Sinai for forty days to test their hearts. God wanted them to see the condition of their own hearts. For God already knew the condition of their hearts. He wanted them to see for themselves that they were not worthy of the promise land nor His rest that He had planned for them.

God acts on behalf of those who wait on Him. We should never be unwilling to wait on God. For waiting on God increases our faith in Him and in His word. Waiting also demonstrates our dependency and trust in God.

DEVELOPING YOUR FAITH

Scripture teaches us that faith comes by hearing the word of God repeatedly. To develop our faith we must use it. God will sometimes create circumstances in order to stretch our faith. God knows that without faith it is impossible to please Him. Therefore, He helps us to develop our faith with real life situations. God wants His children to overcome obstacles in the world. Each time a child of God faces a trial that he overcomes, his faith increases. Moreover, everything that we do, must be done in a spirit of faith. The Bible teaches us that the just must live by faith and not by what we see or feel. We can always ask God to help us with our faith and He said that He would never leave or forsake us.

Remember that God is the author and finisher of our faith. He will finish what He started with each of His children. Scripture teaches us that a little faith is sometimes all that we need. In *Luke 17:6* the Lord said, *"If you have faith as a mustard seed, you can say to this mulberry tree 'Be pulled up by the roots and be planted in the sea, and it would obey you."* God will sometimes allow grief, disappointment and sorrow to come into our lives to strengthen our faith. When a child of God applies faith in every circumstance that he is faced with God is pleased.

God Loves You

Everything that God desires for His children is based on His love for them. His children do not lack in anything that is good for them. For this is a promise of God that His children can depend on Him for all their needs. God imparts knowledge to His children through His word. Can you imagine the lack of knowledge we would have if we did not have the holy Bible? We have the freedom to read the Bible anywhere in America and not be punished by the government or the authorities like some others countries. The word of God has many promises for His children to look forward to and expect. History has proven that not one word of God's promises has ever failed. God's children can always depend on the promises and the word of God. In fact, God and His word are the only things that we can count on that will not fail.

God is always imparting knowledge to His children through His word and through the Holy Spirit. One of the greatest acts of love is the death of Jesus on the cross. God made a way for His children to receive eternal life and to be with Him forever by sending His only Son to die so that we could escape eternal damnation.

God made more blessings available to His children who would consider the needs of the poor. In Africa alone, over four thousand children die from unsafe water daily, and over twenty-four thousand that die from starvation each day. The need for food alone among the poor is staggeringly high. In the book of **Psalms 41:1**, it tells us *"Blessed is he who considers the poor; The Lord will deliver him in time of trouble. The Lord will preserve him and keep him alive, And he will be blessed on the earth; You will not deliver him to the will of his enemies. The Lord will strengthen him* *on his bed of illness; You will sustain him on his sickbed."*

God wants us to take care of the poor, because we are His servants who have been called to do His will and it is the will of the Father that no one starves to death. There are people all over the world who are perishing for one reason or another. It is love for others that will bring an end to starvation. There is enough food on the earth to feed all people. If only there were enough people who cared as much as necessary to extend sufficient help and resources to those with needs, we could save lives by ending hunger.

LIVE A LIFE THAT IS PLEASING TO GOD...

Chapter Four

Your Commitment To Love Others

"Just as the Son of man did not come to be served, but to serve, and to give His life a ransom for many."   *Matthew 20:28*

COMMIT TO LOVE OTHERS

When we do not love one another, we fail to obey one of God's commandments. As a result, we are not living a life that is pleasing to God. How can a child of God expect to receive any of God's promises if he is disobedient to God's commandments? Will God overlook this sin of disobedience of a child of His? The Bible clearly tells us that God is a God of love. He wants love to exist in the hearts of His children, and He wants us to love others.

When we love others as we love ourselves, we are doing the will of our Father. He is pleased with us.

EDIFY ONE ANOTHER

Scripture tells us in **Romans 14:19,** *"Therefore let us pursue the things which made for peace and the things by which one may edify another."* The Bible tells us *"Let each of us please his neighbor for his good, leading to edification"* **(Romans 15:2).** It is pleasing to God when we share the things of God with others; especially things that God has revealed will edify others. Kind words are encouraging and uplifting when spoken to others. People need to hear words of kindness and uplifting especially if they are going through a period of orchestrated adversity. Remember this is the perfect time to remember the promises of God that will give us hope. I think we all have moments like this at times. King David had moments when he was down hearted and the Bible tells us that he would encourage himself with the word of God. Are we to do the same as David did?

SERVING OTHERS

God did not call us to *be served* by others. We as God's chosen ones were called to serve others. For this is the will of God. The need of people today is overwhelming and God's way for them to be served is through His servants who are willing to be obedient. God's word promises to bless those who are a blessing to others. There are so many people today that are suffering from the basic needs of life and they cannot help themselves for one reason or another. There are thousands of people today in foreign countries who do not have clean water to drink. There are thousands of people who do not have enough food to stay alive today in foreign countries. These are just some of the needs that exist somewhere on earth every day. We who are the children of God must ask Him what is it that we can do to help those who cannot help themselves. This need is not God's alone; it belongs to every child of God. Remember if you are a child of God, you are an ambassador and a representative of God. This means that if we cannot physically help because the need is in a far country, we can always pray for the needy and poor. *Psalm 41:1* teaches us how to help the poor and the needy. Remember when you are serving the poor; you are actually glorifying God through Jesus Christ our Savior.

The Bible tells us that in the last days men would become lovers of themselves and not others. It is not pleasing to God when we think only of ourselves and not others. This is the way of the world, which is totally opposite of the ways of God.

When Jesus was on the earth, He was always considerate of the needs of others. He never turned down anyone who needed His help. He showed love to others wherever He went. These acts of love and kindness that he demonstrated were examples for the children of God to follow. Jesus was following the second commandment of God, which states *"You shall love your neighbor as you love yourself." **Matthew 22:39***

Scripture tells us in **Philippians 2:3-4,** *"Let nothing be done through selfish ambition or conceit, but in lowliness of mind let each esteem others better than himself. Let each of you look out not only for his own interest, but also the interest of others."* God sees everything good or bad. Moreover, there is nothing that He does not see. For everything is before Him and nothing is hidden from him.

Chapter Five

Meditate On His Word

"This book of the law shall not depart from your mouth, but you shall meditate in it day and night, that you may observe to do according to all that is written in it. For then you will have good success." **Joshua 1:8**

"Your words I have hidden in my heart, that I might not sin against you." **Psalms 119:11**

MEDITATE ON THE WORD OF GOD

There are countless blessings to us when we meditate on the word of God. Only God really knows all the blessings that a child of God receives as he allows the word of God to enter his mind and remain there. The Bible tells us in **Hebrews 4:12,** *"For the word of God is living and powerful, sharper than any two-edged sword, piercing to the division of soul and spirit, and of joints and marrow, and is a discerner of the thoughts and intents of the heart."* Scripture also teaches us that the word is like medicine for our health. Therefore, when we take in the word of God we are actually ingesting medicine that is good for us. Remember, meditating on the word of God affects the mind and body. God has commanded us to do this for it is good for us because it brings blessings in our life.

Meditating is a form of reflecting on what you have read. It allows the material to become a part of your mind and brain. I used a form of mediating on college material when I was in college and found that it was an ideal way to internalize what I wanted to stay in my head. I am certain this was why I was able to recall volumes of material and achieve high grades on final exams at Morehouse College. Therefore, when God tells His children to meditate on His word He understands the powerful benefits you will receive.

GOD WILL GIVE YOU GOOD SUCCESS

Good success can only come from God. The world has its own definition of success and it is quite different from the success that God Promises to His children. The world defines success as the accomplishment of some worthwhile goal or the attainment of something sought after. God's idea of success for His children is for them to seek Him for directions in their life and allow Him to guide them step-by-step, to a place where He has already planned for them to be. Remember what God told Jeremiah about what He had planned for him? *"For I know the plans I have for you, declares the Lord, plans to prosper you and not harm you, plans to give you hope and a future." **Jeremiah 29:11 (NIV)*** No child of God can create a plan for his life without the help of God, which will exceed the plans God has for him.

Remember God is the only One who has the power to give increase to any endeavor. Any achievement that we try to make in life without God is only a gamble and surely a waste of valuable time. I wasted many years trying to be successful according to the world, when I did not have a relationship with God. Now that I have learned my lesson, I think that I am well qualified to warn you that God's way is much better. I have repeated this lesson to my son Kevin on more than one occasion. There was no one available to tell me that the world's way is not the right way. God's way is the only way for His children to live their lives.

God only wants good success for His children. It grieves Him when His children will not listen and go their own way in life. He knows that there will be suffering and disappointments later in life when His children do not choose His way.

Remember the world does not know God or His ways. The Bible tells us that God's ways are foolishness to the world. This is the reason the world does not follow the teaching of the Scripture.

You Are His Workmanship

We are called, through the workmanship of God, to be used for His Glory. We are called to perform good deeds on the earth. Whenever we are serving God, we are in line with Scripture and God gets the glory. Jesus was sent to earth by God to serve and to be a ransom for us. He did not come to be served. We are to follow His example and ask God what He would have us to do to serve Him. If we imitate what Jesus did on the earth, we will serve others just as Jesus did. We will visit the poor, help to heal the sick, and feed the hungry.

Jesus was compassionate and sympathetic to everyone who had a need. He did not overlook anyone. He was a blessing to everyone he met.

God wants His children to be just like Jesus was when he was on the earth. Jesus demonstrated love and kindness everywhere he went. Even when he was not accepted or understood, he continued the assignment God had given him. He allowed no one to stop him from doing everything God instructed him to do.

During your life on earth, you will see many opportunities to assist others who are in some kind of need. The Scripture tells us if we see our brother in need and have the material things that could help him yet we do not assist him, then how does the love of God exist in us. We should never refuse to help someone who is in need when we have the means to do so. Remember God sees everything that we do and do not do. If we say no to helping someone else, how can we go to God when we have a need with a clear conscious? Will our conscious condemn us? I do believe that God will sometimes test our heart and send someone to us with a need to see if we will fulfill the need of someone else. The Bible says that we shall reap what we have sown. If you have been negligent in giving to others in the past, why not repent and ask God for forgiveness and begin to help others when you have it to give. If you do not have it to give, God will not hold it against you. However, if you have it and refuse to give to someone who has a need, God will remember what you did and He could refuse a blessing to you when you ask Him for help.

Make sure our deeds please God in every way. God sees everything that we do on a daily basis. I am sure that He is watching each of His children to see what kind of deeds or services are offered by them. God will be the judge of all of our deeds whether good or bad.

Scripture teaches us about the soundness of our work. In *1 Corinthians 3:14* *"If anyone's work which he has built on it endures, he will receive a reward."*

Jesus is no longer walking the earth to be of service to people in need. Jesus was our example as to what we as God's children should be doing to help others. We are to do the services that Jesus did by helping others when we can help. Jesus said to His disciples before He left the earth that they would do the things that He did and greater things they would do because He was going to the Father in heaven. There will always be work to do on earth, more work to do than people will be available to perform.

BE ACCOUNTABLE TO GOD

The Bible tells us that God is observing the good and the bad deeds of every person on the earth. He is especially concerned about the deeds of His children. Because everyone will have to give an account of every deed performed. God will reward every good deed that was done to help the poor and those deeds that were performed to help those who could not help themselves. God is the provider of everything for His children. His word says that He will supply all of our needs according to His riches in Christ Jesus. When we have a need, God uses people to get help to us with the supply. He knows who to use to get help to us. There is nothing He cannot do, and He is always willing to hear the prayers of His children.

It is always wise to pay close attention to the voice of God and talk to Him concerning your availability to be used by Him if He needs you to be of help to someone.

It pleases Him to know that you are willing to be of service to Him when a child of God has a need. Remember that God never has a need for anything Himself. For God is all sovereign and all sufficient.

I believe one of the best ways to be accountable to God is to serve God and let Him know that you will follow Him. In addition, you will be honored by the Father.

His children have needs and God knows the needs of His children even before they ask. Some of God's children are poor and without substance because of lack of knowledge. Some of God's children are perishing for a lack of knowledge. God wants all of His children to read and study His word for knowledge and to ask Him for understanding, for He is always willing to give His children understanding because the Bible tells us in all that we get, get understanding.

LIVE A LIFE THAT IS PLEASING TO GOD...

Chapter Six

He Is Our Life

"If anyone serves Me, let him follow Me, and where I am there My servant will be also, If anyone serves Me, him My Father will honor." **John 12:26**

Jesus Is Your Life

According to Scripture, Jesus is our life and without Him, we cannot have life. We can merely exist at most. It is the Spirit of God in us that gives life. God created us to be His children and He wants the best for us. He paid the ultimate price by sending Jesus Christ to die for the sins of the world. Those who accepted Jesus as their personal Savior received the Gift of Salvation. Therefore, we are not our own. We were purchased for a price—we belong to God. He is our Father in heaven, He cares for us and provides for us.

God has work for each of His children on earth. Jesus was our example when He walked the earth. However, the children of God will do the work that Jesus did when He walked the earth. Now we are the servants of God through His Son Jesus Christ. God has an assignment for each of His children. Each of our assignments will be revealed by God in time. In *Matthew 6:33* it tells us *"Seek first the kingdom of God and His righteousness and all these things shall be added to you."* What things? The promises of God, your assignment and your rewards.

The life that we have in Jesus must be pleasing to God. Life is about the will of God and not just about us. Remember Jesus is the vine, we are the branches, he that abides in Jesus, and Jesus in him, will produce much fruit for without Him you can do nothing. This teaching can be found in *John 15:5.*

We must live a committed life to God to be pleasing to Him. With the help of the Holy Spirit, we can live a life that is the will of God. Everything that is good for us God said that He would provide, if we continue to abide in Jesus who is our life. It is wise to include Jesus in every aspect of our life because He promised to be there always. He will never leave or forsake us. Life will sometimes bring us things that we will not understand. If we continue to abide in Jesus, He will see us through every adversity that life has to offer. Never try to handle life without Him because He wants us to trust in Him and not ourselves. In **Proverbs 3:5-6** it tells us *"Trust in the Lord with all your heart, and lean not to your own understanding; acknowledge Him in all your ways and He will direct your path."* God wants to be a guide for all of His children and He does not want His children to go through life on their own strength.

God wants a personal relationship with each of His children and this relationship begins with Him training His Children in the ways of God. No child of God can train himself on the ways of God. *In Hebrews 12:11* it teaches us, *"Now no chastening seems to be joyful for the present, but painful; nevertheless, afterward it yields the peaceable fruit of righteousness to those who have been trained by it."*

ONLY GOD CAN GIVE INCREASE

As a child of God, we must understand that it is God who is our blessing. We may be able to do many things for our families and ourselves, however, it is God who gives us the strength to perform these things. All of God's children should want success that can only come from Him and this is good success, which is different from the success of the world. The success from God and the world's success are explained in chapter five. Do not ever fall in the trap of seeking success the world's way because God will not honor it. God only honors what

35

is done through faith, without faith, it is not pleasing to God. The Bible tells us that God wants to give His children everything that is good for them. He wants to give them an abundance of things that will enhance their lives. Remember in *John 10:10* Jesus said, *"The thief does not come but to steal, and to kill, and to destroy. I have come that they may have life, and that may have it more abundantly."*

Only God has the power to give His children an increase in whatever they do. We can plant and we can water, but only God has the power to increase what is planted. Scripture tells us that without Him, we can do nothing and life will demonstrate this fact to every believer in time. So why waste time and try to do things without God. He is always waiting for His children to rely on Him and not themselves. This is the kind of love that God has for us, it is love that is beyond our understanding and comprehension. He wants His children to always abide in His Son so that they can always be productive and have good success. God wants us to have all things in life that are good for us. If it is not good for us, he will not give it to us no matter how often we ask Him. He knows what is good for us and what is bad for us. We as the children of God do not always know what is good or bad for us.

God expresses His love for us in *Romans 8:32* "He who did not spare His own Son, but delivered Him up for us all, how shall He not also with the Son freely give us all things."

PRACTICE SELF CONTROL

It is said that he who has mastered his own body is done with sin. The ability to master one's self is self-control, according to the fruit of the Spirit. For self-control is a virtue that most people do not possess. For this must be learned and practiced through maturity. Lack of self-control is responsible for much of the lawlessness, crime and wars in the world.

To be pleasing to God we must practice and live the fruit of the Spirit which is listed in **Galatians 5:22** *"But the fruit of the Spirit is love, joy, peace, longsuffering, kindness, goodness, faithfulness, gentleness, self-control."* When we are practicing and living according to these virtues God is pleased with us. Remember Jesus in His walk on earth demonstrated these qualities in His life. Could it be that King David was operating in lack of self-control when he lusted after Bathsheba? Joseph's brothers were guilty of a lack of self-control when they decided to throw Joseph into an abandoned well.

Cain lost self-control when God did not receive his offering and he became angry to the point he killed his brother Abel.

PUT ON THE WHOLE ARMOR OF GOD

The Scripture teaches us that the Devil is roaming the earth trying to find someone whom he may devour. We as God's children have the protection of God. However, the Bible warns us to wear the whole armor of God at all times. It is for our own protection against the wiles of the evil one. The Devil led Jesus into the wilderness to tempt him, but Jesus used the word of God to defeat the devil by saying, *"It is written, Man shall not live by bread alone, but by every word that proceeds out of the mouth of God."* The devil told Jesus to command that some stone become bread. Jesus used the sword of the Spirit, which is the word of God to defeat the Devil. This teaching can be found in **Luke 4:4**

We do not wrestle against flesh and blood, but against principalities, against powers, against rulers of the darkness of this age, against spiritual hosts of wickedness in the heavenly places. For the full protection of your body, you should have your waste girded with the truth of the breastplate of righteousness, your feet with the preparation of the gospel of peace. The shield of faith to protect you from the fiery darts of the wicked one. The helmet of Salvation and the sword of the Spirit, which is the word of God. Once we have the full armor of God we are protected against anything the Devil can bring our way. **Ephesians 6:12-17**

Chapter Seven

Your Commitment To God

"Commit your works to the Lord and your plans will succeed. "

Proverbs 16:3 NIV

GOD SENT HIS WORD TO HEAL THEM

The children of God who cry out to Him can be healed by the power of His word. They must stand on the promise of *Isaiah 53:5* that states, *"But He was wounded for our transgressions, He was bruised for our iniquities, the chastisement for our peace was upon Him, and by His stripes we are healed."* God has already given the believer the healing that is needed in his body. Whenever there is a symptom of any illness, we must never claim we are sick, what we should claim is the promise of the healing that was already given to us by the stripes that Jesus received for us. He took the pain of the stripes many years ago for our healing today. All we have to do is to believe His word that this promise is true and receive the benefit of our healing. Scripture teaches us that not one of the words of any of His promises has ever failed. In the book of Joshua, it tells us that *"Not one of all the Lord's good promises to the house of Israel failed; every one of them was fulfilled." Joshua 21:45 NIV*

God's word is something that His children can always depend on. However, we must have faith to operate in this promise of God. Scripture teaches us that when we come to God, we must believe that He is, and that He will reward those who diligently seek Him. It is highly imperative that we believe all of the promises of God, which are the word of God. When we come to God, we are coming to Him to believe Him. Why should a child of God come to him with doubt that what he says is not true? If a person has problems believing the promises of God, why accept the Bible as being true? I have talked to people who have said that they believe some parts of the Bible but they do not believe other parts of the Bible. If a person thinks like this, why bother to read the Bible at all. How can one have faith if he is going to pick and choose what to believe in the word of God? This type of thinking comes from a person who has a condition of the heart. This type of thinking prevented many Israelites from entering the promised land. Their hearts were callous and they refused to change after being in the wilderness for forty years. God allowed them to perish in the wilderness because of their disbelief. I do not have the answer for anyone who does not believe God other than him having a condition of the heart. Nevertheless, there are many people who fall in this category of nonbelievers.

We as children of God have the privilege to call on our Heavenly Father for whatever we need. He has always promised to answer His children when they call on Him. In *Psalm 91:15*, it tells us that the Lord says, *"He shall call on Me and I will answer him; I will be with him in trouble; I will deliver him and honor him, with long life I will satisfy him. And show him My Salvation."*

LOVE YOUR ENEMIES

We as children of God must love our enemies because this is a commandment of God. We love our enemies because we want to obey God, not that we desire to love our enemies. There is a reward in obeying God and we obey God because we love Him. The Bible teaches us in *Luke 6:35*, *"But love your enemies, do good, and lend hoping for nothing in return, and your reward will be great and you will be sons of the Most High. For He is kind to the unthankful and evil."* We must not treat our enemies the way they treat us. For when we treat our enemies, the way they treat us, this is not pleasing to God. For we are acting the same way they are acting. God always wants us to act in love. In *Matthew 5:44* it tells us, *"But I say to you, love your enemies, bless those who curse you, do good to those who hate you, and pray for those who spitefully use you and persecute you."* As children of God, we will not have to defend ourselves because the Lord has said that He will handle any situation, persecution or mistreatment from our enemies. In *Deuteronomy 28:7* it tells us, *"The Lord will cause your enemies who rise up against you to be defeated before your face; they shall come out against you one way and flee before you seven ways."*

In *Psalm 119:98,* God's word tells us that when we are careful to obey Him, He will make us wiser than our enemies.

GIVE CHEERFULLY

When we give to the work of the Lord or when we give to the poor and the needy, God will always bless us. God's word says in *Proverbs 28:27, "He who gives to the poor will not lack, but he who hides his eyes will have many curses."* When we give to the work of God, we should always give cheerfully, not grudgingly, because God loves a cheerful giver. When we give cheerfully, God is pleased and when we do not give cheerfully, God is not pleased.

The Scripture teaches us in *2 Corinthians 9:7, "So let each one give as he purposes in his heart, not grudgingly or of necessity; for God loves a cheerful giver."* When we give cheerfully, God gives us more seed. We can sow more seed than before and receive a larger harvest. God will give us more opportunities to sow and do good for this is pleasing to Him. When God gives us seed to sow and we give to those who are in need, it is counted to our giving as being faithful with what He gave us. If we are faithful with a little, we can be trusted with much.

LIVE A LIFE THAT IS PLEASING TO GOD...

Chapter Eight

Choose Life

Many years ago, God spoke to Zechariah and told him that He would come to the earth and dwell among His People.

"Sing and rejoice, O Daughter of Zion! For Behold, I am coming and I will dwell in Your midst," says the Lord. **Zechariah 2:10**

CHOOSE LIFE

When a person chooses Jesus, he is choosing life, because Jesus is life. The fullness of life is in the embodiment of the Son of God. God gives each one of us the choice to choose Jesus or not to choose Him. We have been given this choice according to **Deuteronomy 30:19.** The Lord tells us *"I call heaven and earth as witnesses today against you, that I have set before you life and death, blessing and cursing; therefore choose life, that both you and your descendants may live."* Not to choose Jesus is a curse and to choose Him is life and blessings. When a believer obeys the word of God and His commandments, he is showing his love for God and he is demonstrating the life of Jesus that dwells in him. This is the life that God intended for His children to live. There are many people who are living a life of cursing, because they choose to live a life without Jesus. You can see the curse on their lives by what is taking place in their lives in the neighborhoods and on television. God's word is true and it will reveal itself to those who are paying close attention. The world will not accept the Bible's account that cursing will come upon those who reject Jesus, who is life. These people do not have the knowledge of the word of God. It is very clear in *Hosea 4:6* when the Scripture tells us *"My people perish for the lack of knowledge."* In essence, people are dying because of what they do not know and what they do not understand. Understanding comes from studying God's word and knowing His precepts (God's Rule) and being obedient. If anyone is in Christ he is a new creation; the old has gone, the new has come! This new creation is from God Himself. He is reconciling us to Himself. This is His plan he has had for us before the foundation of the earth. You were chosen to be God's child long before you entered your mother's womb. God choose

His children to do the work of His kingdom and to be ambassadors and representatives for Him. This is one of the reasons why God must train each of us to walk in His ways. Based on what Jesus did for us, in that God made Jesus, who knew no sin, to be sin for us so that in Him we might become the righteous of God.

DELIGHT YOURSELF IN THE LORD

God wants His children to find joy, pleasure, and satisfaction in our relationship with Him. Our personal relationship with God is what God desires from each of His children. The first of the Ten Commandments support this statement, because it says that we must love God with all our mind, heart, and strength. God wants to be everything to us, and He wants us to place nothing before Him. Not even our spouse or our children whom we love very much. God wants to give His children the best of everything and He does not want His children to live in lack of anything that is good. Remember the promise that was made by God *IN* **Romans 8:32,** *"He who did not spare His own Son, but delivered Him up for us all, how shall He not with Him freely give us all things?"* Just think, If God gave His Son for us to have eternal life, what else will He do for us? This proves just how much God loves His children. God's children should never take this act of love that God performed lightly. It is the greatest act of love that has ever been demonstrated in the history of man, and we, as children of God should never question the fact that we should offer our bodies as a living sacrifice to God.

When we think about the goodness of God and what He has done for us our hearts should rejoice with gladness and with thanksgiving. Everything that a child of God will ever need is in God Himself. He is our sole provider and care keeper. It is said that God fills and occupies every atom and every atom is at His command. When God speaks, there is nothing that can resist His will. In the book of Genesis the first chapter and third verse, Then God said "Let there be light." And, there was light. Why was there light after God spoke? The answer is God controls everything in the universe, including all people and all things. There is nothing that is outside of His control.

The first step in delighting one's self in the Lord is to obey God and keep His commandments. If you really love God, you will obey Him and wait on Him for His promises. When you diligently seek Him and set your mind on His word, in time He will reveal Himself to you in His own way. The peace of God will permeate throughout your mind and heart. You will discover that there is no peace like the peace of the presence of God. It surpasses all human understanding. The peace of God is a promise and His promises are only for His children and not the world. Remember the world is an enemy of God, and the things of God are foolishness to the world.

We as God's children should always keep our minds on the Lord at all times. In this way, we are delighting ourselves in the Lord also. Furthermore, meditating on God's word at the same time, will give us a new heart that is pleasing to God. Success will come to God's children, who do what the word of God says. In the book of *Joshua 1:8*, it tells us, *"Do not let this book of the law depart from your mouth; meditate on it day and night, so that you may be careful to do everything written in it. Then you will be prosperous and you will be successful."*

JESUS YOUR SENIOR PARTNER

Every child of God should make a decision to abide in Christ always, which means to make sure you are always depositing the word of God into your mind and you are walking in the ways of God. When you do this, there is a personal relationship that exists between you and Jesus. You have made Jesus your partner and this can be supported by Scripture in *John 15:5,* which says, *"I am the vine and you are the branches. He who abides in Me, and I in him, bears much fruit; for without Me you can do nothing."* A child of God is wise to include Jesus in even the small things in his or her daily life. We should also include Jesus when facing major decisions that will eventually arise in our lives.

Do you realize that God made His children to depend on Him? The world does not receive or understand this because the world does not know God or His ways. In most cases, the children of God must be taught how to depend on God. We cannot depend on the school system to teach God's children how to depend on God. Just who is responsible to teach God's children how to depend on God? It is supposed to be the leaders in the body of Christ that should teach the children of God how to depend on Him.

Take Jesus with you wherever you go. You can do this by just talking to Him in a low voice and say Jesus I recognize you as my senior partner. Will you accommodate me to the meeting that I have today. I need you to assist me. For with you I think I can be productive (be fruitful), thank

You Father for hearing me. After you have prayed this prayer, say to yourself, "I believe" for about three or four times. This will add to your faith and pay very close attention in the meeting, because God will be working on your behalf.

Chapter Nine

Fear God (And Nothing Else)

"Blessed is the man who fears the lord, who delights greatly in His commandments, His descendants will be mighty on earth, the generation of the upright will be blessed. Wealth and riches will be in his house, and his righteousness endures forever."   **Psalm 112:1**

"For God did not give us a spirit of fear, but of power and of love and of a sound mind."   **2 Timothy 1:7**

FEAR GOD

Scripture teaches us in **Psalm 103:11,** *"For as the heavens are high above the earth, so great is His mercy toward those who fear Him."* The mercy of God is upon the children of God who are fully committed to His ways. God's protection, His love and His care follow His children wherever they may be. There are just two things in life that will conclude the duty of all of God's children. One is to fear God and the other is to obey His commandments. The world does not receive the teaching of God neither do they walk in His ways. Those who are in the world that have rejected Jesus have a reason to fear the future because the future is unknown to them. They are not sure what will happen to them. How can the people of the world who have rejected Jesus Christ have peace about their future? They do not understand the things of God because they do not know Him. If they do not know Him, how can they call on Him when there is trouble in their life? God's children are instructed to fear God and obey Him. However, the children of the world are not instructed to fear anything else. God gives His children the spirit of power and of love and a sound mind. Every child of God should come to the realization that God is his strength and power and no one can do any harm to him.

Psalm 27:1 teaches us, *"The Lord is my light and my salvation; whom shall I fear? The lord is the strength of my life; of whom shall I be afraid?"* All believers should know that God would never leave them or forsake them wherever they may be. This is a promise of God and not one word of God's promises have every failed. Remember what God told Joshua? This teaching was not only for Joshua but it is for the children of God today. *In Deuteronomy 31:6,* "*Be strong and of good courage, do not fear nor be afraid of them; for the Lord your God, He is the One who goes with you; He will never leave you or forsake you.*"

When a child of God is faced with some kind of trouble or danger, a choice has to be made. He can choose to have faith by believing the promise of God or he can choose to not believe God's promise and be fearful. His choice should be to have faith in what God's word says.

For the word of God can never fail. It will always prevail.

We must remember that the word of God is alive and it is powerful and sharper than any two edged sword. When we take the word of God in us, it becomes alive in us also, as we meditate on it day and night. Could it be also that in time we will have the mind of Christ because of the power of the word of God? In *Galatians 4:19* it says, "*My little children, for whom I labor in birth again until Christ is formed in you.*"

SEEK TO ENTER THE KINGDOM OF GOD

After salvation, the most important step for the new believer is to develop a personal relationship with God by seeking His kingdom. This is a direct instruction of God to all believers. In the kingdom of God is the place where all the promises are located and so is God's rest for His children. In *Matthew 6:33* it states, "*Seek first the kingdom of God and His righteousness, and all these things shall be added to you.*" The righteousness of God is in the children of God who have received Jesus Christ in their lives. We are the righteous of God because of Jesus. The world does not recognize the righteousness of God and neither can it know righteousness. The righteousness of God is foolishness to the world. The kingdom of God is a government that exists on the earth and it dwells on the inside of every committed child of God. Jesus is the head of this kingdom, and this government is on the shoulder of Jesus Himself. In the book of **Isaiah (9:6),** it tells us, *"For unto us a Child is born, unto us a Son is given; and the government will be upon His shoulder. And His name will be called Wonderful, Counselor, Mighty God, Everlasting Father, Prince of Peace."*

No unrighteous person can enter the kingdom of God. In **1 Corinthians 6:9-10** it states, *"Do you not know that the unrighteous will not inherit the kingdom of God? Do not be deceived neither fornicators, nor idolaters, nor adulterers, nor homosexuals, nor sodomites, nor thieves, nor covetous, nor drunkards, nor revilers, nor extortioners will inherit the kingdom of God."*

Chapter Ten

Confessing Jesus

"Therefore whoever confesses Me before men, him I will also confess before My Father who is in heaven."   **Matthew 10:32**

"Because he loves me ,' says the Lord, 'I will rescue him; I will protect him for he acknowledges my name. He will call on me and I will answer him; I will be with him in trouble, I will deliver him and honor him. With long life I will satisfy him and show him my salvation."   **Psalm 91:14-16 NIV**

CONFESSING JESUS

Scripture tells us to call on Jesus when we are facing trouble and He will save us. *Joel 2:32* The name of Jesus is the highest name of all names. Even demons tremble at the name of Jesus. Demonic forces flee at the name of Jesus. There is power in the name of Jesus. We as children of God should always lift up the name of Jesus whenever we have the opportunity. In the book of Revelation, Scripture tells us that if anyone confesses the name of Jesus before men He would confess their name before the Father in heaven. He is our help in time of need no matter what trouble we find ourselves in or where we may be, He is there for us. We may be in the hospital, in a foreign country, in a remote area in Africa, or in the Amazon forest, Jesus is there also. We must simply remember to call on Him. For Jesus is Lord everywhere in the universe. His children will never be without Him. This is a promise of God for all of His children. With Jesus at our side, we do not have to fear anything or any person.

Remember, there is no person or persons that can stand up to God and defeat Him. God is the potter and everything He made is the clay. Can the clay say to the potter, "I am greater than You?" God made everything, and there was nothing made that He did not make. Thus, everything is subject to Him. For He controls everything in the universe. The children of God should also boast in the name of Jesus, because He is our life and without Him, we would not have life. We would only exist without the Spirit of God. There would be no hope for the children of God without Jesus. We would be as a lost world that exists, headed for damnation. This is why Jesus is everything to a child of God. Moreover, this is why we as children of God always lift up the name of Jesus whenever we get the opportunity.

ALWAYS ABIDE IN JESUS

"These things I have spoken to you, that in Me you may have peace, in the world you will have tribulations; but be of good cheer I have overcome the world." **John 16:33**

"I am the vine, you are the branches. He who abides in Me, and I in him, bears much fruit; for without Me you can do nothing. If anyone does not abide in Me, he is cast out as a branch and is withered; and they gather them and throw them into the fire, and they are burned. If you abide in Me, and My words abide in you, you will ask what you desire, and it shall be done for you. By this My Father is glorified, that you bear much fruit; so you will be My disciples." **John 15:5-8.**

When a child of God keeps the commandments of God, he is abiding in God and in His love. We must remember that without Jesus we cannot bear fruit. However, with Him, we can bear much fruit and this is what the Father wants because this is the way He is glorified through His Son Jesus. When we abide in Jesus and His word abides in us, we are in partnership with God. Jesus is the senior partner and the child of God is the junior partner. With Him, we can do all things and without Him, we cannot do anything. If by chance we accomplish something without Him, it will turn into ashes. So why bother trying to do anything without Him. For His word says we cannot accomplish anything without Him.

Jesus is greater than anything we know in life. He is powerful and knows about every situation we face. He wants His children to depend on Him for everything in life. Yet, in some cases, we choose not to depend on Him.

He may watch us fail miserably. Nevertheless, He is always there to get us back on our feet and try it the next time His way. For His way is always the best way. You must remember, his way is never the world's way. Try to pay close attention to the way Jesus instructs you the next time.

Life is almost impossible to live without Jesus. So many of God's children live without Jesus and they suffer needlessly in doing so. Nevertheless, God is a loving God who will always forgive us and show us His way to get us back on track. All of God's children get off track every now and then. We learn from God, by falling down, getting back up, and doing it the next time according to God's way. God does not scold us for making mistakes. He just gives us another chance and we learn from our mistakes.

When we abide in Jesus, and He abides in us, Scripture teaches us that we can ask God for anything and He will do it. If we have love for our brother, we know that God lives in us. What is more, the love of God has been perfected in us. We attract God's best to us when we do the things that please Him. When we fear Him and obey His commands this is what pleases God.

Servants Of God

The Bible tells us that we should love God with all our mind, heart and strength. Next, we should love our neighbor as we love ourselves. We are serving God when we help others who cannot help themselves. God has called His children to be servants of others. There are many people on this earth who have needs and they look to God for the answer to their needs. God has commissioned His children to help people who are in need. God's servants are His eyes, ears and hands on the earth. We do the things that God has told us to do in His word. When Jesus was on the earth, He spent three years serving people who needed help. He fed the poor, He healed the sick, He preached to those who needed to hear the gospel. He was always tending to the needs of the people. He is the Son of God and He is a servant of God. God instructs His children to love others. There will always be people who have needs everywhere we go. If we love others, we will want to help them wherever we can. Jesus was our example when He was on the earth. We must do the things that Jesus did when He was on the earth. The child of God must always be thinking of how he can help those who cannot help themselves. For this is what is pleasing to God and He notices every good deed that is administered by His children. For there is no good deed that goes unnoticed by God. If you want God's attention, begin to give to the poor in a systematic way. He will honor you for doing what you are doing and that is having consideration for the poor. A certain centurion named Cornelius who lived in Caesarea was noted for giving gifts to the poor and he got the attention of God. God responded to Cornelius by sending Peter to his house. God sent salvation to Cornelius and his household by way of Peter. While Peter was speaking to Cornelius and his household, the Holy Spirit fell on everyone present. And, Peter commanded them to be baptized in the name of the Lord Jesus Christ.

Chapter Eleven

God Owns Everything

"The earth is the Lord's and all its fullness, the world and those who dwell therein." **Psalm 24:1**

"The silver is Mine, and the gold is Mine,' says the Lord of hosts." **Haggai 2:8**

"Yours, O Lord, is the greatness, the power and the glory, The victory and the majesty; for all that is in heaven and in earth is Yours." **1 Chronicles 29:11**

GOD OWNS EVERYTHING

Scripture tells us that God made everything and He owns everything on the earth. Man is just a temporary custodian or caretaker of property. Thus, God will hold man accountable for stewardship of His property. God also owns man because He created man and will also hold man accountable for what he does with his body. Our bodies are the temple of God and Scripture tells us that if we destroy this temple, He will destroy us. God made everything to please Himself. God created everything with a plan in mind. God wanted a family that He could relate to so He made man in His own image, so He could have children on the earth.

According to the Bible, God has a specific plan for each of His children. *"For I know the plans I have for you,' declares the Lord, 'plans to prosper you and not harm you, plans to give you hope and a future."* **Jeremiah 29:11 (NIV)**

Scripture also teaches us in **I Corinthians 6:19-20,** *"Do you not know that your body is the temple of the Holy Spirit who is in you, Whom you have from God, and you are not your own? For you were bought with a price; therefore glorify God in your body and in your spirit, which are God's."*

God is in control of everything on the earth, even the Devil and his demons are under the control of the Almighty God. God only allows the Devil to go but so far. For He has a boundary around what the Devil can do. Do you remember the story of Job? The Devil complained to God that there was a shield around Job and he could not penetrate this shield. With God's permission The Devil attacked Job and his family and his property. However, God would not allow the Devil to touch

Job's life. Later God restored Job with double what he had loss.

WEALTH COMES FROM GOD

All God's children should know that all wealth comes from God. He owns it all and the world has possession of most of the wealth that is in the earth. Scripture tells us in *Ecclesiastes 2:26,* *"To the man who is pleasing Him, God will give wisdom, knowledge and happiness, but to the sinner He will give the task of gathering and storing up wealth to hand over to the one who pleases God."* According to this promise, The wealth of the world will not remain in the hands of the ungodly. It will be transferred into the hands of God's children. Only God can control how and when this will occur. Therefore, this wealth that is in the hands of the ungodly is temporal and not permanent. The children of God must remember that God made an oath with our ancestors years ago, and God will always keep his covenants and His promises. This oath can be found in *Deuteronomy 8:18,* *"And you shall remember the Lord your God, for it is He who gives you the power to get wealth, that He may establish His covenant which He swore to your fathers, as it is this day."* Wealth will come to the believer who is living a life that is pleasing to God. It must happen because of the promise that God has made. Moreover, not one word of the promise of God has ever failed.

God wants His children to have the best of everything that is good. He will see that His children do not lack anything that is good. Remember God knows what is good for us, we do not always know. So do not expect that God will give you just material things, because He always knows what is best for you.

The Bible tells us that God has pleasure in the prosperity of His children, However, we should have as our aim to receive from God when we have as our primary goal to advance the kingdom of God and not have a selfish goal only for ourselves. Remember, we are to be the servants of God and not just ourselves. As children of God, we must always demonstrate love for others just as Jesus did when He was on the earth. God will give His children nice things, but He wants us to consider the needs of others also.

ALWAYS ASK IN FAITH

As the children of God, we should always ask Him for what we need in a spirit of faith. For faith is the only way we can please God. We must learn how to live by faith and believe that God wants the best for us. Just as a good parent wants the best for her child, we must believe that God is the same. For He wants, the best for us, and this is supported by Scripture. God gave us His best when He gave us His Son Jesus Christ. If He gave us His best when He gave us Jesus, He will also give us His best today. We represent His children on earth and God is not glorified when we look like there is lack in our lives. God wants to bless all His children and He will bless us when we are obedient to Him and pleasing to Him. In addition, He is blessing us even when we are not aware of His blessings.

God does not have to use money to bless His children. There are other ways He can bless us such as protection and health, peace and joy and long life. All these things are a form of wealth. The other part of wealth such as money will be a part of the blessing from God also. However, it will happen in His timing and not our timing.

Because he made a covenant with the fathers many years ago, God will always keep His promises and His covenants. God's word tells us throughout Scripture that we should ask Him for what we want. He promised to do what we ask, if we ask in the name of Jesus. Whenever we ask God for anything, we must ask Him in faith, and we must continue to ask Him until He gives us an answer. The Bible says if we have the confidence to know that whatever we ask is according to His will He hears us. Moreover, if He hears us whatever we ask will be ours. If what we ask Him for is not in His will, He does not hear us. We must make sure what we ask of God is in His will. If what we ask is not good for us, He does not hear us. God knows the future and if what we ask of Him is not good for our future, He will not grant us our request because He wants the best for us in the future not just for today. God can always give us more than we ask if what we ask is in His will. Scripture tells us in **Ephesians 3:20,** *"Now to Him who is able to do exceedingly abundantly above all that we ask or think, according to the power that works in us."* We must remember that if we doubt God we will not get what we ask of Him. We must believe that we have already received what we ask for. We must ask God for what we want according to His word and His word tells us in **James 1:6-7,** *"But let him ask in faith, with no doubting, for he who doubts is like a wave of the sea driven and tossed by the wind. For let not that man suppose that he will receive anything from the Lord."* Remember we as children of God must not ask Him for what we want just one time. Scripture teaches us that we must ask and keep on asking until God gives us what we are asking for. Could it be that God wants to see if we really want what we are asking for. If we really want something from God, is it worth asking over and over again? I believe that God wants His children to believe that He will give them what they ask if they ask in faith without reservation. This is the type of faith He wants His children to have. We should never doubt God before we ask Him for anything. We must believe that He wants us to have good things and that He will provide those things that are good for us. In addition, when we ask God for what we desire, remember to ask always in the name of Jesus.

Chapter Twelve

He Gives Us Power Over Sin

"The God of Israel is He who give strength and power to His people."

Psalm 68:35b

SHOULD YOU ASSOCIATE WITH THE UNGODLY?

"Do not be unequally yoked together with unbelievers. For what fellowship has righteousness with lawlessness? And what communion has light with darkness."

2 Corinthians 6:14

The Bible refers to the unbeliever as the ungodly. In addition, God has instructed His children not to associate with the unbeliever. Scripture is clear on this point in the book of **Psalm 1:1-2,** *"Blessed is the man who walks not in the counsel of the ungodly, nor stands in the path of sinners, nor sits in the seat of the scornful; But His delight is in the law of the Lord, and in His law he meditates day and night."* An unbeliever does not recognize the commandments of God and therefore he is not bound to them. The conduct of the unbeliever is in line with the world's way of thinking. In addition, the world does not have the knowledge of God because the world does not know God. If a child of God is trying to lead an unbeliever to Christ, it is ok to be in the company with him. For this is pleasing to God, because this could lead to salvation for the unbeliever. God considers all unbelievers as lawless people who have rejected Jesus Christ as their Savior. If God leads one of His children to witness to an unbeliever then by all means follow the leading of the Holy Spirit and do just that.

The conversation of the unsaved people of the world and God's children are unequally yoked. There is no common ground in a situation like this. Can an unsaved person talk about the things of God who he does not know or understand? The wisdom of the world and the wisdom of God are completely different. We as children of God must love those who are unsaved, but we must not compromise with them on any subject of Scripture. The Bible tells us that God will train all children who come to Him and teach them His ways. *Hebrews 12:11.* God will also scour (clean) every believer that He receives. *"For whom the Lord loves He chastens, and scourges every son whom He receives."* **Hebrews 12:6.** God considers all unbelievers as unclean in the sense that they have not been chastened or scourged by Him.

All of God's children are called righteous because of their relationship with Jesus Christ. They have been made righteous because of the sacrifice of the blood of Jesus. The righteousness of God is foolishness to the world and the ungodly. The world does not understand the power or the will of God. The Spirit of God does not dwell in the ungodly. Therefore, they do not have the knowledge nor the understanding of what is pleasing to God.

WALK IN HIS WAYS

King David instructed his son Solomon to walk in the ways of God. In *1 King 2:3* it states, *"And keep the charge of the Lord your God; to walk in His way, to keep His statues, His commandments, His judgments, and His testimonies as it is written in the law of Moses, that you may prosper in all that you do and wherever you turn."* We as the children of God must not follow the ways of the world because the world does not have the love of God. Moreover, the world does not teach the love for one another. The children of God must walk in love and righteousness as God's word teaches us. When we do, God is pleased because we are being obedient to His command to love others. Remember, the ways of God does not make sense to the world, but the ways of the evil one do. The world has adopted the ways of the Devil and has rejected the ways of God. The Bible tells us that the Devil is the ruler of the world and therefore His ways are accepted among people who are not saved. In *2 Corinthians 4:4* it states, *"Whose mind the god of this age has blinded, who do not believe, lest the light of the gospel of the glory of Christ, who is the image of God, should shine on them."*

My fellow saints, here is a truth, the Devil's commands and his precepts are observed by the world system. Moreover, they make sense to the world, because the world knows the ways of the evil one. Scripture supports this statement in **Revelation 12:9:** *"So the great dragon was cast out, that serpent of old, called the devil, who deceives the whole world."*

It is not easy to be a child of God because the world system is against Christianity. The world promotes fame and fortune, not good character and love for others. The world is in total opposition to the things of God. The world is controlled by money, power, and lust. The love of money, power, and lust in the world is the root of the evilness of the world. God's children are taught to love others and not money or power. God rewards His children by giving them peace, joy and happiness when they are obedient to Him. Peace, love, and joy can only come from God. These are some of the promises of God to His children.

Chapter Thirteen

The Will Of God For Your Life

"Let us hear the conclusion of the whole matter: Fear God and keep His commandments, for this is man's all." **Ecclesiastes 12:13**

FOR THIS IS THE FULL WILL OF GOD TO MAN

God's ways are higher than our ways and His thoughts are higher than our thoughts. It is the will of God that His children trust Him in every aspect of their lives. We make our plans daily, but it is God who promises to guide our steps. We are never alone. He is there directing our every step. The Bible teaches us this truth in **Proverbs 16:9;** it says, *"A man's heart plans his way; but the Lord directs his steps."* In other words, the Lord is always there to guide us on our way. This is the love of the Father, who is our Shepherd and we are the sheep. He makes sure we do not get off track. Therefore, He leads us in the direction that we should go. We must believe that He is always with us; and this is why we do not have to fear.

God also directs our steps because He has our best interest in mind. God has promised His children so much and He wants them to have all He has promised. So God is determined to keep you safe and in good health. Remember, He gave you Jesus, which was the greatest act of love anyone could bestow on another. We should ask ourselves, what more is He willing to do for those who love Him? Every child of God is in His plan and it is the will of the Father to see that plan come true. In *Jeremiah 29:11,* God talks about the plan He has for His children. We should seek Him to know the plan that God has for each of us.

SPEAK PLEASANT WORDS TO OTHERS

"Pleasant words are like honey comb, sweet to the soul, and health to the bones."   **Proverbs 16:24**

God commands His children to love others as they love themselves. If we love others, we will only say pleasant words to them. We can surely hurt the spirit of another person if we say unkind and demeaning things to him or her. Some people have a difficult time getting over the words spoken to them by a close family member or friend. Many times hurtful words are never forgotten by others so it is always best to use self-control when speaking to others . We can always find something good to say to another person if we pay close attention.

Remember God loved us before we loved Him and he wants us to love others as He loves us. Jesus was our example on the earth. He was always kind and thoughtful to everyone He came in contact with.

We as the children of God should never say anything unkind to our parents. Scripture teaches us to honor and respect our parents. If we honor and respect them, God will give us long life. This is a commandment from God and it is the first command with a promise. Do you know that if a person is having a bad day, their spirit can be uplifted, if we speak cheerful and pleasant words to them. Remember God is watching everything we say and do to others, and He does not forget.

Our words have power and can be damaging to another person when spoken. It is best to think about the consequences of the words we use before we speak. Ugly and demeaning words are not supposed to come from a person who has the Spirit of God in them. Do not be deceived for God is not mocked, if we speak unkind words to another, the same words that we spoke will come back to visit us from another source.

Let us always speak words of love and kindness to others because it is pleasing to God. When we do not speak words of kindness, we will be reprimanded by God Himself. For God will always correct His children and show them what is righteous.

STEWARDSHIP RESPONSIBILITY

God owns the earth and everything that dwells in it. He even owns you and me. Scripture tells us that God has given the earth to men. God expects man to use clear judgment in taking care of the earth just as you would take care of anything that was entitled to you for a period of time. God placed everything on this earth for man's use and habitation. Scientists are not aware of any other planets that are suitable for human existence like the earth. Man is held accountable to the stewardship of the earth by God Himself. God holds man responsible for everything He has put in his care. For example, a father has the responsibility to care for his family. He also has the responsibility to lead, and love his family. The man should be the priest of his household. He should lead the family in the knowledge of the word of God. Both parents, however, have the responsibility to bring up the children in a way that is pleasing to God. Scripture teaches us that God hates divorces in the family. Moreover, we know that there are negative consequences to a broken home. The children seem to pay the biggest price when there is a divorce in the home. When both parents are committed to God, a divorce is unlikely to occur in the family.

Lastly, the wealth that God allows His children to acquire must be used in a wise way that is pleasing to God. He expects the parents to use sound judgment and good stewardship in use of all wealth that comes in the household.

LIVE A LIFE THAT IS PLEASING TO GOD...

Chapter Fourteen

Jesus Our Confidence

"For the Lord will be your confidence, and will keep your foot from being caught."   **Proverbs 3:26**

"Beloved if our heart does not condemn us, we have confidence toward God."
                                            1 John 3:21

"Let us hold fast the confession of our hope, without wavering, for He who promises is faithful."   **Hebrews 10:23**

JESUS OUR CONFIDENCE

Our confidence should never be in ourselves, but in the power of Jesus Christ. He is our strength and our hope. For without Him we cannot accomplish much. He lives on the inside of every child of God, and every child of God exists inside of Him. Scripture teaches that we are one with Him. We as the children of God should always boast about the knowledge of Jesus our Savior. We should never boast about ourselves, because without Him we can do nothing on our own.

As children of God, we should not have any confidence in this world system. The world system will bless its own, but it will not bless the children of God because the children of God do not walk in the ways of the world. The world system does not promote righteousness, because righteousness is from God. The children of God are righteous in the world, but they are not of the world. If the children of God were of the world, the world would accept them as its own.

Scripture tells us to place our confidence in Jesus who sits on the right side of the throne of God. He is the advocate of every child of God. He is interceding to God for every saint that dwells in Him. We should be steadfast in the confidence we have in Jesus Christ our Savior. Every chance we get we should confess the name of Jesus to men, and Scripture tells us that when we do this, Jesus will confess us before the Father.

There will be opportunities for the child of God to lift up the name of Jesus to someone who does not know Him. There are many lost souls in the world and we are the servants of God who must represent Him and lead others to God, when the Holy Spirit prompts us to do so. Scripture tells us that we can be bold on the things of God, and this boldness comes from God Himself. *Ephesians 3:12* tells us, " *in whom we have boldness and access with confidence through faith in Him.*" We as saints should know that we can approach God with any need or request that we may have at any time. *Hebrew 4:16* states, *"Let us therefore come boldly to the throne of grace, that we may obtain mercy and find grace to help in time of need."*

JESUS WAS WOUNDED FOR YOU

It is the will of God that all of God's children receive healing for their bodies. A promise of God states that the children of God are already healed. Jesus Christ paid the price of every believer's healing through the stripes He received during His crucifixion. This was not a pretty site, to behold. However, it was the will of the Father to allow it to happen for the benefit of His children's health and well-being. Our benefits for the suffering of Jesus at His crucifixion are our peace, our healing, and the forgiveness of our sins. God allowed the crucifixion to happen because He loves His children and He wanted the best for them. Scripture supports this in *Isaiah 53:5*, *"But He was wounded for our transgression, He was bruised for our iniquities; the chastisement for our peace was upon Him, and by His stripes we are healed."*

In order to have these blessings on our lives, we must be in good standing with God by living a life that is pleasing to Him. The Bible tells us that to please God we must obey Him and keep His commandments. The price that Jesus paid on the cross is something that every child of

God should keep in his heart and never take it lightly. Never forget that He did this when we were not His children. We were of the world and sinners in the world. In fact, we were enemies of God. Yet He died for us that we might become His children.

CAST ALL YOUR CARES ON JESUS

Scripture tells us to cast all our cares and burdens on Jesus for He cares for us. He said that His burden is light and His yoke is easy. He knows exactly what we can bear for He knows all things and nothing is hidden from Him. Jesus wants to be everything to us and He wants to carry all of the weight of everything that is too much for us to bear. Scripture says *"Come to Me, all you who labor and are heavy laden, and I will give you rest. Take My yoke upon you and learn from Me, for I am gentle and lowly in heart, and you will find rest for your souls. For my yoke is easy, and my burden is light."* **Matthew 11:28-30**

His plan for you as His child is not to add to your burdens, but to give you abundant life. The abundant life offered to those who seek Him is the best of all He has to offer—the Promises he made to Abraham. As a child of God, we too are heirs to the same.

No matter what our circumstances, we must rejoice in the Lord and give thanks for the hope that is within us. For God has promised, *"Be anxious for nothing, but in everything through prayer, supplication and with thanksgiving, let your request be known to God, and the peace of God that surpasses all understanding will guard your hearts and minds through Jesus Christ."* **Philippians 4:6-7**

God is concerned about the welfare of every believer. He teaches us how to have peace of mind through trust and faith that He will guard our hearts from being troubled amid a world of turmoil and unrest. Remember, only God can give us the peace, joy, and hope He promised.

LIVE A LIFE THAT IS PLEASING TO GOD…

Chapter Fifteen

Our Hope For The Promises Of God

"For all the Promises of God are yes, and in Him Amen, to the Glory of God through us." **2 Corinthians 1:20**

"By which have been given to us exceedingly great and precious promises, that through these you may be partakers of the divine nature, having escaped the corruption that is in the world through lust. " **2 Peter 1:4**

"Not one of all the Lord's good promises to the house of Israel failed; everyone was fulfilled." **Joshua 21:45 NIV**

Throughout Scripture, it tells us that God wants the best of everything for His children. He demonstrated the depth and breadth of His love for His children when He allowed His Son to die for the salvation of His children.

Scripture teaches us that God has made promises of wondrous gifts to those of us who seek and trust in Him, His abundant gifts will always be greater than any gift from our mortal parents.

As you seek the wisdom of God and grow in your relationship with Him, He will prepare you to receive His promises. His promises are both conditional and unconditional. Conditional promises require some action or change in behavior on the part of the believer. We earn His unconditional promises through our spiritual relationship, and faith and belief in Him.

The children of the world do not qualify for the promises of God because they are not the children of God. The children of the world have rejected the saving grace of Jesus Christ and therefore they are not in the family of God.

There were requirements to enter the promise land. One of the requirements was that the Israelites had to change from the old ways they had learned in Egyptian bondage.

The requirements to enter the promise land under Moses' leadership and the requirements to receive God's promises today are the same. The world can be considered as Egypt and both are considered to be in bondage. Egypt was bondage of a physical slavery and the world is bondage of sin slavery. Only God can give freedom to both of these two kinds of slavery. No Hebrew had the power to free himself from the slave bondage of Pharaoh. Likewise, no person can free himself from the bondage of sin of this world. Only God has the power to free a person from the sin of this world. Once we are free from sin by God Himself, God will begin to refine our character and change each person that comes to Him. God must change each person to fit in the family of God. This process will begin with a cleaning process of God's children.

The Israelites of the first generation that left Egypt refused to change so God would not let them enter the promise land. Only two people made it into the promise land. Joshua and Caleb were the only two people that made it. Moses did not enter the promise land because He disobeyed instructions from God to speak to the rock to get water for the Israelites to drink. He did not die in the wilderness, for God buried Moses Himself.

In God's preparation of His children for His promises, He will correct, mold, chasten and refine their character. He will do whatever it takes to get us to change to be members of His family. Scripture tells us, *"Now no chastening seems to be joyful for the present, but painful, nevertheless, afterward, it yields the peaceful fruit of righteousness to those who have been trained by it."* **Hebrews 12:11**

Remember, if we endure chastening, God deals with us as sons, for what son is there whom a father does not chasten? If you are without chastening, of which all have become partakers, then you are illegitimate and not sons. God loves us and He corrects and cleanses every son whom He receives. God wants His children to be like His Son Jesus and that will require sanctification to continue the renewing process of the believer.

DON'T BE ANXIOUS ABOUT ANYTHING

There seems to be a common thread that runs through the minds of most people, and that is most people prefer not to wait for something they want. We live in a microwave society that promotes instant gratification. Some people are programmed that waiting is not ideal even at the cost of receiving something of less quality or at a higher price. However, Scripture tells us to be anxious for nothing. The Scripture is telling us that self-control should play a role in our character at all times. In **Philippians 4:6-7,** *"Be anxious about nothing, but in everything through prayer supplication and with thanksgiving let our request be known to God and the peace of God which surpasses all understanding will guard our hearts and minds through Jesus Christ."* Remember, whenever you find yourself in the mindset of being anxious about anything, this is not the way of God and He tells us that self-control is a better way to be. God is a God of peace and He will give us peace when we ask for it. When we obey God and act in a way that is pleasing to Him, he wants to give us His best. As illustrated in **Ecclesiastes 2:26:** *"For God gives wisdom and knowledge and joy to a man who is pleasing in His sight; but to the sinner He gives the work of gathering and collecting, that he may give to him who is pleasing before God."*

God will require that His children wait on Him. When a child of God obeys Him by waiting, the Bible tells us that God is good to those who wait on Him. Therefore, it is pleasing to God when we exercise self-control and be willing to wait for God's timing.

ALLOW GOD TO TRAIN YOU

God has a plan for each of His children. A plan to give them a future and hope. This is the love of God for all His children. Scripture tells us that God wants better things for His children than what our earthly fathers want for their children. This claim can be supported in *Matthew 7:11.* God will train every child that comes to Him from the world system. He wants to change each child to His way of living. Thus, the way to bring about change is through training. In *Hebrews 12:11* it tells us, *"Now no chastening seems to be joyful for the present, but painful; nevertheless, after-ward it yields the peaceful fruit of righteousness to those who have been trained by it."* God wants to prepare His children to receive His promises and His blessings, so He trains them His way so that they are pleasing to Him. His training is an act of love and caring, nothing else. He is not punishing His children when they come to Him from the world system. He wants to change them from the world's way to His way, which is a better way of life.

Remember, God had to change the Israelites when they were freed from slave bondage under the rule of the Egyptian government. God wanted to change the Israelites to His way because they only knew the life of slavery. God wanted to be their father and provider of everything. The Israelite children would not change. God refused to let them go into the promise land. Their hearts were hardened and they were a rebellious nation. All of the Israelites of the first generation that came out of Egypt died in the wilderness except Joshua and Caleb. All 20 year old and younger of the second generation went into the promise land. It was God's plan for all of the Israelites to enter the promise land.

It was not His plan that so many Israelites perish in the wilderness. This was their choice that they perish and not a choice of God Himself. The Bible said that the Israelites were a stiff necked and hardhearted people that were ungrateful and indifferent.

Chapter Sixteen

It Is All About God

"Jesus said to Him, 'If you believe, all things are possible to him who believes".   ***Mark 9:23***

LIFE IS NOT ABOUT YOU

Life is all about God and very little about you. God is the sustainer of life and without Him, we would fail to exist on this earth. Life does not depend on what we think or do because the only thing we can control is how we respond to our circumstances. God is in control over everything in the universe. God placed us here on the earth to have a family that He could be in relationship with. If you have received Jesus Christ as your Lord and Savior, you are a child of God. He expects you to be a servant of His to assist others who have a need and cannot help themselves. Jesus was a servant of the people and He served God by serving people. Jesus told His disciples that they would do the same things He did and greater things they would do because He would go to the Father.

God does not have a need. There is nothing in Scripture that says God has a need. However, there are God's children on the earth who have needs daily and they cry out to God for help. The Israelite's children were in bondage for over four hundred years. They cried out to God and He sent Moses to lead them out of Egypt. Nevertheless, God had to prepare Pharaoh's heart. Therefore, it was God who orchestrated the exodus of the Israelites out of Egypt. This exodus of the Israelites into the wilderness was all about God and not about Moses for Moses was an instrument of God.

NEVER DOUBT GOD

Scripture tells us that we cannot please God if we doubt Him. We must believe God when we come to Him. Why come to God if we are not going to believe Him? This point is clear in **Hebrew 11:6:** *"But without faith it is impossible to please God. For he who comes to God must believe that He is, and that He is a rewarder of those who diligently seek Him."* There are people who do not believe God for one reason or another. They may say something like, "If only God would show me a sign or miracle I would believe." Remember God showed the Israelites ten miracles and they still did not believe God. Their hearts were callous and evil to the point where they became rebellious and disobedient. Many of these Israelites died in the wilderness because they refused to change. The point I am trying to make is that when a person wants to see miracles from God, it is just like the doubting Thomas in the Bible.

It is enough for me to believe God and have faith in Him by just observing the heavens and the earth. When I see a baby born, this is a miracle in itself. What else do I need to see to believe God? David said, *"The heavens declare the glory of God and the firmaments shows its handiwork."* **Psalm 19:1.**

The Devil can deceive many people not to believe in God but the Devil is not the total blame. For it is also the condition of the heart of man. Scripture tells us in **Revelation 12:9,** *"So the great dragon was cast out, that serpent of old, called the Devil and Satan, who deceives the whole world; he was cast to the earth, and his angels were cast out with him."* The Devil and his angels are doing evil things to hurt people on earth. He is killing, stealing, and destroying people wherever he can. The Devil hates the children of God, but God has a shield around those who obey Him. Remember, God protects His children at all times.

God wants His children to believe Him and never doubt Him. The Devil has discredited and polluted the word of God. This is why God's children must abide in Jesus and He in them. Then the Devil cannot penetrate this relationship.

GOD GIVES GRACE AND MERCY

God blesses His children in either of two ways— sometimes by mercy and sometimes by grace. When He blesses us by giving us specific instructions, this is a blessing of grace. The lady who had an issue of blood for twelve years had received instructions from God to touch the garment of Jesus and she would be healed of the blood disease. As soon as she touched Jesus' garment she was healed in the same hour. This was a blessing of grace, which means that you have to follow instructions to receive the blessing. Paul had an ailment and he went to God with a request to have this thorn in his side removed. Paul wanted God to heal him with an act of mercy. Paul went to God three times and each time God refused to heal his ailment. Paul believed that a messenger of Satan was sent to buffet him to prevent him from being exalted above measure. This report can be found in *2 Corinthians 12:9: "And my grace is sufficient for you, for My strength is made perfect in weakness."* God was telling Paul to operate in His grace, and use what He taught him for his own healing.

Today I see on television many acts of mercy where God blesses others who are in trouble and there is no way out of the trouble unless God saves them. When these persons call out to God in distress, God makes a way for the person to be saved. God has an obligation to His children because they are His family. He has promised to keep them safe. Yet, there are times when God will have mercy on those who are not His children. The Bible tells us that He will have compassion and mercy on whomever He chooses.

WHEN WE DIE TO SIN

When a person has received Jesus in their life and has committed his ways to the will of God he has died to sin. The Bible teaches us in **Romans 6:3** *" Or do you not know that as many as were baptized into Christ Jesus were baptized into His death?"* In **Romans 6:7-9,** we learn *"For he who died has been freed from sin. Now if we died with Christ, We believe that we also will live with Him."* We are now a new creation in Christ; our past has been erased by the grace of God forever. Therefore, sin has no more power over us.

Chapter Seventeen

Spiritual Living Verses Carnal Living

"I say then walk in the spirit, and you shall not fulfill the lust of the flesh."   **Galatians 5:16**

There are only two ways any person can live, spiritually or carnally. When a child of God is living a life according to the Spirit of God, he is living a spiritually life and this is pleasing to God. In addition, when a child of God is living a spiritual life, his body is dead to sin. If a person is living a life according to his flesh, he cannot please God. Moreover, the Spirit of God does not dwell in him, and he is spiritually dead. When the flesh is enmity against God, the things of God do not make sense to him. Remember, no one can live in the Spirit of God and live carnally at the same time.

Every believer who lives according to the Spirit, who are in Christ Jesus, there is no condemnation to them because their life is pleasing to God. Therefore, anyone who is in Christ he is a new creation and old things have passed away; behold all things have become new. *2 Corinthian 5:17*

Carnal living leads to death and Spiritual living is life through Jesus our Lord. Scripture teaches us in **Deuteronomy 30:19,** *"I call heaven and earth as witness today against you, that I have set before you life and death, blessing and cursing; therefore choose life, that both you and your descendants many live."* Spiritual living is essentially abiding in Jesus, and living an obedient life through the word of God.

LINK YOURSELF WITH JESUS

When a believer is abiding in Jesus and Jesus is abiding in him, you are linked with Him. This is the only way a believer can produce anything that is pleasing to God. This is like a partnership arrangement. In *John 15:5,* it tells us *"I am the vine, you are the branches, he who abides in Me and I in him, bears much fruit* (very productive)*; for without Me you can do nothing."* When linked with Jesus in partnership, we will not only bear much fruit we will live a life that is peaceful and filled with joy. The Bible tells us that we can do all things through Jesus Christ who strengthens us. We are at our best when linked with Him, and He with us.

This is the will of the Father, and this is what pleases Him. God Himself chose you from the world, because you responded to His calling. No one can choose God, for God chooses us by drawing us to Him. Therefore, God decides who will be His children, and it is not about us at all. Scripture teaches us in *John 15:16-17, "You did not choose Me, but I chose and appointed you that you should go and bear fruit, and that your fruit should remain, that whatever you ask the Father in My name He may give you. These things I command you, that you love one another."* Thus, we have the answer to why God chooses us.

He chose us and appointed us to go and bear fruit. As we bear fruit for God, we can ask Him for anything in Jesus name; and He promised to do it. The condition to this promise is we must bear fruit for God. What kind of fruit does God want His children to bear? The answer is the *fruit of the Spirit.* This is what God wants His children to produce: love, patience, goodness, kindness, longsuffering, faithfulness, gentleness, peace, joy and self-control. These fruits are what God wants us to produce. Moreover, as the children of God produce these fruit He will prune us so that we will bear more fruit. If a child of God does not bear fruit at all, he becomes cast-off like a dead branch on a fruit tree.

Therefore, we see what happens to the children of God who do not produce any fruit. God wants His children to be like His Son Jesus. For Jesus produced much fruit by demonstrating the fruit of the Spirit. Thus, we are to do the same as He did, bear much fruit.

To learn more about the fruit of the Spirit, refer to **Galatians 5:22.** Memorize the nine parts of the fruit of the Spirit and keep them in your heart. For this is pleasing to God.

The life of a child of God joins with Him in every aspect of his daily living. In **Deuteronomy 30:20,** it teaches us *"That you may love the Lord your God, that you may obey His voice, and that you may cling to Him, for He is your life and the length of your days; and that you may dwell in the land which the Lord swore to your fathers, Abraham, Isaac and Jacob, to give them."*

BELIEVE GOD'S WORD

Believing God's word is the same as believing in God Himself. For God cannot be separated from His word. Remember the Word of God was with God in the beginning. In **John 1:1** it states, *"In the beginning was the Word and the Word was with God, and the Word was God. He was with God in the beginning."* As you see, one cannot separate the word of God from God. For they are the same. The Holy Spirit will reveal this revelation to us as we grow in the things of God. However, we receive it in faith and not with intellect. For the intellect is of the things of the world. The Holy Spirit cannot be intellectually discerned and neither can the intellect know God. The intellect is of the flesh and not of the spirit, and this is why the flesh and the spirit are contrary to one another. When someone hears the word of God, one must decide whether to believe if what is heard is true or false. If God has not shine light into the darkness of their heart, they will not believe. Remember it is not about any person believing God's word. It is about God drawing that person to Him. No person can come to God, unless God Himself draws him. Remember only God can select His children, for He already knows who they are. He knew from the beginning.

Jesus performed many miracles during his time on the earth to get people to believe that God actually sent him, to believe that he was in the Father and the Father was in him. In addition, Jesus would say to the people if you do not believe me, believe the work that I do. Jesus wanted those who He came in contact with to believe in Him. Jesus asked the people in *John 14:10*, *"Do you not believe that I am in the Father and the Father in Me ? The words that I speak to you I do not speak on My own authority; but the Father who dwells in Me does the works."*

GOD'S WORDS HAVE POWER

God made us in His image and after His likeness, which means we have some of the attributes of God. Moreover, the Bible teaches us to imitate God as dear children. We are told to imitate Jesus, as He was our example while He was on earth. He said that we can do the things that He did, and greater things because He would go to the Father. So basically, we as God's children are supposed to be God's representative just as Jesus was God's representative while He was earth. Jesus healed people who needed healing. He taught His disciples to do the same things. To healed the sick, give sight to the blind, open the ears of the deaf and raised the dead.

He sent the disciples off to another city to do the things they were taught to do. The disciples return with good reports of what had happened. They marveled at the result of the power of their words, which brought about healing and casting out demons. The disciples imitated Jesus and they received the same result that He did. They believed that their words had the same power as Jesus words. Moreover, they did not doubt the power of their words.

We can also imitate Jesus just as His disciples did and get the same result, if we do not doubt what we say. Believe it because God's word tells us we can. It is our faith that will make the difference. Know that it is the power of God's word that will do the healing and not us. The healing power comes from God through our faith, which allows the healing to take place.

We have been given the authority through Jesus Christ to speak and expect results. In **Mark 11:23** it tells us *"For assuredly, I say to you, whoever says to this mountain, 'Be removed and be cast into the sea,' and does not doubt in his heart, but believes that those things he says will be done, he will have whatever he says."* The believer should understand that he must not use the power of his words in the wrong way. He should never say that he does not feel well or he thinks he is going to be sick. The power of what is being said could work against him. Remember Jesus said that you will have what you say if you believe in what you are saying. The Bible tells us that we are already healed by the stripes that Jesus received on our behalf. When a troubling symptom exists in our bodies that could indicate existence or onset of an ailment, we must claim what the Scripture says about our healing. We should say that we are healed in the name of Jesus, because He paid the price for our healing and we give Him thanks for it now.

We should repeat this over and over again until the symptom leaves.

Chapter Eighteen

It Is Not God's Will That Any Should Perish!

"The Lord is not slack concerning His promises, as some count slackness, but is longsuffering toward us, not willing that any should perish, but come to repentance."   *2 Peter 3:9*

It Is Not God's Will That Any Should Perish

The knowledge of the word of God and the benefits of His promises are what every believer should keep in his heart. The lack of knowledge is more damaging to the body of Christ than anything else I can think of. No one can act on something that he does not know. What you do not know can cause you to perish and Scripture supports it in *Hosea 4:6* *"My people (God's children) perish for the lack of knowledge."* If a beautiful plant is placed in the sill of a window to receive sun light and is not given water regularly it will perish. However, when the Bible speaks about a child of God perishing it could take years. I do not care to imply that I have the authority to know how long it will take any person to perish; only God knows. God wants His children to have the knowledge of His word and to be obedient to His word. Why? He loves us and He is concerned about us living a life that is pleasing to Him. Knowing God's word is what He instructs His children to do. When a child of God does not know the word of God can they have understanding? Without understanding, how can a child of God follow His instructions? Will we not perish if we do not understand the things of God? In *Hosea 4:14b* of the New International Version it tells us, *"A people without understanding will come to ruin!"*

The knowledge of the word of God is crucial and it is the responsibility of every child of God to know His word. I believe that a lack of knowledge of the word of God and the lack of understanding of the word of God are both an epidemic in the world today. We cannot blame the pastors and other leaders because the Bible clearly says, study to show yourself approved of God. In *2 Timothy 2:15* it states, *"Study to show thyself approved unto God a workman that needs not to be ashamed rightly dividing the word of truth."* We must understand this very clearly that we will not be able to hold someone else to blame for our lack of knowledge when we are face to face with God. The word of God is like a lifeline. It contains everything we need to know about how God wants us to live. God's word is our life and God gives every child a choice. The choice is very clear that He wants us to choose life and not death. This teaching is found in **Deuteronomy 30:19-20,** *"This day I call heaven and earth as witnesses against you that I have set before you life and death, blessings and curses. Now choose life, so that you and your children may live and that you may love the Lord your God, listen to His voice, and hold fast to Him , for the Lord is your life, and He will give you many years in the land He swore to give your fathers, Abraham, Isaac, and Jacob."* God is giving instructions to His children with a promise on how to live. He is telling us what will happen if we do not choose Jesus.

TRUST GOD

"O Israel, trust in the Lord, He is their help and their shield. O house of Aaron, trust in the Lord; His is their help and their shield. You who fear the Lord, trust in the Lord; He is their help and their shield." **Psalm 115:9**

"Every word of God is Pure. He is a shield to those who put their trust in Him." **2 Samuel 22:31**

It is the will of God that all of His children fully trust Him. God showed the Israelites many miracles to get them to trust Him. However, these miracles did not foster a desire for the Israelites to change from their rebellious ways. They still refused to change from their ungodly ways. God would not allow them to enter the promise land.

God does miracles and wonders today. Every time a baby is born, it is a miracle of God. Whenever there is a healing, it is a miracle of God. Even with all the miracles that God demonstrated in order for the Israelites to see so they could trust Him, it did not work for all the Hebrew children. Many of them died in the wilderness because they did not believe God and they did not trust Him.

When we trust in the Lord, it means that we are willing to wait on Him. If a child of God will not wait, it tells me that this child of God does not love Him. The Israelite children did not love God, and they did not trust Him. If they had loved God and trusted Him, they would have waited for Moses to come down from the mountain when God was finished with him. Instead, they decided to have Aaron make them a golden calf to worship. This act kindled a fire of wrath in God. They could not have done anything worst. And, this is something that God will not tolerate from His people. Consequently, many Israelites died that very day from their action of idolatry and rebellion

God wants a believer to trust Him and wait on Him. This is something that shows our love for Him. He rewards all believers who wait on Him. When we refuse to wait, it shows what is in our hearts.

Seek To Enter His Rest

"But seek first the Kingdom of God, and His Righteousness, and all these things will be added to you."   **Matthew 6:33**

God's rest is in His kingdom. And at the head of His kingdom is Jesus. The kingdom of God is a government system. This governmental system is within every child of God who has received the Spirit of God through Jesus Christ. Also in this kingdom of God are all the promises of God. Scripture tells us in **Isaiah 9: 6,** *"For unto us a child is born, unto us a Son is given, and the government will be on His shoulders. And He will be called Wonderful Counselor, Mighty God, Everlasting Father, Prince of Peace."* The Kingdom of God is not a place and we do not have to go anywhere to find it. The kingdom of God is on the inside of us. Our bodies are the temple of God, and He dwells in this temple.

Scripture teaches us in **1 Corinthians 3:16,** *"Don't you know that you yourselves are God's temple and that God's Spirit lives in you? If anyone destroys God's temple, God will destroy him; For God's temple is sacred, and you are that temple."* God does not dwell in a temple made with hands, He lives in people.

Originally, God designed the tabernacle and the tribes in Moses' camp built it. The tabernacle was the residence of God and the people knew that God was with them. There was a cloud that settled on the tabernacle and in the cloud was where the presence of God dwelt. The cloud stayed with the people wherever God led them.

The curtain, before the tent of the holy of holies, was torn from top to bottom at Jesus' death on the cross; revealing that God was no longer there. Now, God dwells inside of those who have accepted His Son. You might say that if you are a child of God, you too have a tent where God dwells within. God dwells in this tent. The original tabernacle was in three parts, the outer court, the inner court, and the holy of holies. Our temple (our bodies) is in three parts, the body, the Spirit, and the soul.

Jesus spoke of His body as a temple as He walked through the streets of Jerusalem. He told the Jews, *"Destroy this temple and I will raise it again in three days."* The Jews thought that Jesus was referring to a building, but Jesus was talking about His body and Him being crucified. This teaching can be found in *John 2:19.*

After a child of God has received salvation, the next step for him is to seek the kingdom of God and His righteousness and all these things will be added. *Matthew 6:33.* What are all the things that will be added? The promises of God, His rest and everything else that He wants His children to have.

The first generation of the Israelites died in the wilderness. Joshua and Caleb were the only two that entered the promise lanfrom the first generation. It was the young adults twenty and under) of the second generation went into the promise land and they received God's rest. In *1 King 8:56* it tells us, *"Praise be the Lord who has given rest to His people Israel just as He promised. Not one word has failed of all the good promises He gave through His servant Moses."*

Chapter Nineteen

Be Imitators Of God

"Be imitators of God, therefore as dearly loved children, and live a life of love, just as Christ loved us and gave himself up for us as a fragrant offering and sacrifice to God."   *Ephesians 5:1*

BE IMITATORS OF GOD

God instructs His children to live a life of love just as Jesus lived when He was on the earth. In doing so, we imitate God in the way we live. God demonstrated the epitome of love, when Jesus died on the cross so that we could have eternal life. One could refer to this kind of love as agape love, the selfless love of God for His children. God wants His children to imitate Him, so that when the children of the world see a child of God they will see the light and love of Jesus Christ,.

Let us be a light of Jesus so that others will see Jesus in us. When we do this, we could influence others to want to know Jesus. We are the light of the world and those who are in darkness could be lead to God. Our lives may be the only bible others may ever see. Remember we are the ambassadors of Jesus and we must always be willing to serve. When a child of God assists another person who cannot help himself, or gives to someone in need, he is imitating Jesus Christ. There are so many people hurting in so many ways and as a child of God; we should always be ready to help in a way that is pleasing to God. We are to serve others whenever we can, especially if they are in our center of influence. God expects us to be of service to others, especially to those who cannot help themselves. This is what Jesus did and this is what Jesus said that we should do. When we serve others, we are serving God. And this is what is pleasing to Him.

The children of God have the power of the word of God living on the inside of them. We have been given the authority and the power to speak God's words in the lives of others. This is what Jesus did. If we could not do it, Jesus would not have said that we could. He said that we can do the things that He did and more we because He would go to the Father.

As children of God, we can call those things that do not exist as if they already exist. We have the power to do this if we believe, and do not doubt.

PARTAKING OF THE SUFFERING OF JESUS

"…though he was a Son, yet He learned obedience by the things which He suffered. And having been perfected, He became the author of eternal salvation to all who obey Him." **Hebrews 5:8-9**

"And he who does not take his cross and follow Me is not worthy of Me. He who finds his life will lose it, and he who loses his life for My sake will find it."

Matthew 10:38-39

"If we endure, we shall also reign with Him. If we deny Him, He also will deny us." **2 Timothy 2:12**

Scripture teaches us that God's children will share in the glory of God because of what they suffered. Moreover, if we do not suffer with Him how can we share in His glory? In **Romans 8:15-17(NIV)** it tells us, *"The Spirit you received does not make you slaves, so that you live in fear again; rather, the Spirit you received brought about your adoption to sonship. And by him we cry, 'Abba, Father.' The spirit Himself testifies with our spirit that we are God's children. Now if we are children, then we are heirs-heirs of God and co-heirs with Christ, if indeed we share in his sufferings in order that we may also share in his glory."* God uses our suffering to help teach us the value of obedience. Jesus learned obedience through His suffering. We also learn obedience through suffering. It is God's will for us to suffer like His Son Jesus.

If we claim that we are committed to God, our suffering will support it. Suffering will strengthen our faith and make us strong. Scripture teaches us, *"And the God of grace, who called you to His eternal glory in Christ, after you have suffered for a while, will Himself restore you and make you strong, firm and steadfast. To Him be the power forever and ever Amen."* **1 Peter 5:10.** Therefore, our suffering conforms us to Jesus Christ.

Is it humanly possible to live a life as Jesus lived? Yes, if we allow God to change us through His training. In **Hebrew 12:10-11,** it tells us that our fathers *"disciplined us for a little while as they thought best; but God disciplines us for our good, that we may share in His holiness. No discipline seems pleasant at the time, but painful. Later on, however, it produces a harvest of righteousness and peace for those who have been trained by it."* God trains His children to be holy. It is the training from God that will produce a harvest of righteousness in us.

Hebrews 5:8 tells us the value of suffering. If Jesus had to learn obedience through suffering and He was the Son of God, what do you think God will do to us to teach us obedience? We will have to suffer to learn obedience just like Jesus. It will require suffering to learn the ways of God. When we come to God, we have the world's way in us,. and God will change us to His way, which is living a life of holiness.

FORGIVE OTHERS

The Bible instructs us to forgive others as our heavenly Father has forgiven us of all of our sins. The Bible warns us that if we do not forgive others, God will not forgive us. When we forgive others, we are being obedient and are imitating the Father. This is what the Scripture tells us to do—to be imitators of God as dear children. For obeying God is pleasing to Him. Before we came to God, we were rebellious children of the world. God sent His Son to die and pay our sin debt in full so that we could receive salvation and have eternal life through Jesus Christ. This is the same love of God expressed to all His children.

Scripture teaches us in *Matthew 6:14-15*, *"For if you forgive men their trespasses, your heavenly Father will also forgive you. But if you do not forgive men their trespasses, neither will your Father forgive your trespasses."*

HONOR YOUR FATHER AND MOTHER

As children of God, we are instructed to obey our parents for this is the first command with a promise. Scripture tells us if we honor our parents, life will go right with us and we will live long on the earth. In *Deuteronomy 5:16* it tells us how we are to honor our parents, *"Honor your father and mother, as the Lord your God has commanded you, that your days may be long, and that it may be well with you in the land which the Lord your God is giving you."*

Our parents sacrificed a great deal to bring us up in the world and give us the things we need to make life easier. They did these things because of love and compassion for us. However, we are to return the same love to them and take care of them as they grow older. For this is the right thing to do and it is pleasing to God. We come into the world as babies, dependent on our parents for everything. However, we should leave this world depending totally on God. For it is God who has promised to care for us as we grow older. He promised to give us strength, peace, joy and good health if we have committed our lives to Him long before we became old. This is why God said to seek Him in the days of your youth. Do not wait until you have trouble to seek Him. Where will the faith come from to believe Him for what you need.

Scripture teaches us in *Ecclesiastes 12:1* to, *"Remember now your Creator in the days of your youth, before the difficult days come."* The earlier we begin our faith journey to God, fewer are our years of worry and stress; and greater are the years we will walk by faith and not by sight, knowing God will take care of us.

Chapter Twenty

God Made Us In His Own Image

"Then God said , "Let us make man in our own image, according to our likeness; Let them have dominion over the fish of the sea, over the birds of the air, and over the cattle, over all the earth and over every creeping thing that creeps on the earth." **Genesis 1:26**

And so God did what He said He created man in His own image.

WE ARE THE IMAGES OF GOD

Scripture teaches us that God wanted an earthly family so He created man. He created man to relate to Him and to seek Him.

God wanted children that would love Him above all else. He wanted to be number one in their lives and He would not settle for being number two. Anything short of being number one was a sin of idolatry. When a child of God makes a commitment to place God as number one in his life, God makes a commitment to be a loving Father to provide, protect and take care of every need of His children. God promises to give His children all things that are good for them and more. Scripture teaches us in **Romans 8:32,** *"He who did not spare His own Son, but delivered Him up for us all, how shall He not with Him also freely give us all things."*

This Scripture is telling us that God wants to do more for His children than they could ever imagine. God demonstrated His love for everyone by sending His Son to die for all the sins of the world. God performed this act of love when we were all sinners. If He did this when we were sinners, what will He do when His children become righteous through His Son? Only God knows the answer to this question.

Based on what I have read in the word of God, I can only imagine what God has in store for the children who live a life that is pleasing to Him. Earthly parents want the best for their children and this is nature. If earthly parents give good gifts to their children, how much better gifts will your heavenly Father give to His children who ask Him?

I must admit that I was programmed to think that I would be

better off conforming to worldly ways, rather than trusting in God and doing things His way. The Bible tells us that those of the world have been deceived by the devil to believe the world's way is the better way. **Revelation 12:9** says, *"So the great dragon was cast out, the serpent of old, called the devil and Satan, who deceived the whole world."* The children of God are in the world, but are not of the world; and not easily deceived by the devil. A person that does not have Jesus in his life becomes prey to the deceptions and influences of the devil. Eve, deceived by the devil, foolishly chose not to obey God's instructions. Today, many people continue to do just as Eve did in the garden of Eden. They listen to what the devil says, and reject what God has commanded through His word. They are unaware that the devil speaks through our subconscious, as well as through other people. The Devil also speaks through false prophets and teachers to deceive people.

It is not an easy thing for people to overcome the world's system. The world's system is set in its ways and it will take an act of Jesus to overcome this world's system. But, the children of God have the help of God through Jesus Christ. **John 16:33** teaches, *"These things I have spoken to you, that in Me you may have peace, but in the world you will have tribulation; but be of good cheer, I have overcome the world."*

The main task for all children of God is to seek Him with every fiber of their being. And God will reveal Himself to His children, for this is a promise of God Himself. And God wants to teach His children His ways. And one of His ways is that He wants us to know that the things that Jesus did on the earth, we can do also. And remember the devil and his demons will fight you on this promise, because he knows once you have this knowledge he is finished. This is what Jesus said when He was with His disciples, *"Most assuredly, I say to you, he who believes in Me, the work that I do he will do also; and greater works than these he will do, because I go to My Father."* **John 14:12.**

God's will is for His children to live their lives as Jesus did on the earth. Nevertheless, you may want to ask yourself, why do we not see more of the things that Jesus said we could do if we believe in Him?

God made man for more than one reason. He made man to have a family. He made man to relate to Him. He made man to seek Him. He made man to love and worship Him. He made man like Himself to imitate Him, and He sent His Son as the example to follow. By reading and studying the Word, we come to understand what Jesus did and why. Now we must ask ourselves is it possible for me to do the things that He did? The Bible says we can do the same things He did if we believe in Jesus. The Bible did not say that we must believe in ourselves, but that we must believe in Jesus. It is not about what we can do, it is all about what Jesus can do through us. I have never read anywhere in the Bible where it says "believe in yourself." The world system tells us to believe in ourselves. This teaching goes against Scripture.

This world's teaching "to believe in yourself," rejects the authority of Jesus Christ. It also rejects the need of Jesus Christ in the life of all God's children. God's word tells us without Jesus in our life, we as the children of God cannot do anything. Moreover, without Jesus in our life, we will be in the same situation as the children of the world and that is without hope and without eternal life. Consequently, this is exactly where the devil wants everyone to be--without hope and without salvation.

GOD WILL FIGHT YOUR BATTLE

"The Lord your God, who is going before you, will fight for you, as He did for you in Egypt, before your very eyes, and in the wilderness. There you saw how the Lord carried you, as a father carries a son, all the way you went until you reach the place." **Deuteronomy 1:30-31**

"The Lord shall fight for you and you shall hold your peace." **Exodus 14: 14**

God's plans for His children are in the heart of God. The plan He has for each of His children is shared in *Jeremiah 29:11: "For I know the plans I have for you says the Lord, 'plans to prosper you, and not to harm you, plans to give you a future and a hope."* We as God's children must seek Him to discover His plans for us. There is no other way for the children of God to know His plans for us without seeking Him. If we do not seek Him, what does this say about our interest in His plans for us? Does it mean that we do not believe Him? Does the church teach this concept? If parents do not teach this concept at home, is it because they have never read it in Scripture? Could it be that the parents have never heard the pastor teach it, so they think it is not important to teach it to their children? This is why the Bible says children of God are perishing for the lack of knowledge. Yet, some are perishing because they have rejected the knowledge of the Bible.

The word of God tells us that a child of God never has to worry about trouble in the world. God said that He would always go before the child of God. He is always there to guide and protect His children. This is one of His promises. Scripture tells us that an angel of the Lord encamps around every child of God. *"The Lord encamps around those who fear Him, and He delivers them."* **Psalm 34: 7.** A committed child of God should never fear anything but God Himself. When we fear anything else besides God this is not Scripture.

The attitudes, thinking and behavior of many people in the world are contrary to the teaching of the Bible. And, every child of God should consider that if the world is teaching a concept contrary to the Word, we as children of God must question what is being taught.

The Bible teaches us that God did not give us a spirit to fear anything. In *2 Timothy 1:7* God says *" For I did not give you a spirit of fear but of love and power and a sound mind."* However, there is a spirit of fear that comes from the spirit of darkness in the world; and anything that is from the devil is okay to the world. Fear is promoted in the theaters. The world teaches that it is alright to feel afraid. In fact, the world promotes fear, especially at Halloween. People have learned to be accustomed to fear and in fact, some people enjoy it. Movie producers have cashed in on the promotion of movies that frighten people. We should know that the spirit of fear did not come from God. And, if it did not come from God where did it come from?

Children of God must remember that God is always there to defend and protect them. All we have to do is to call on God for help. He is there at your side even before you call Him. God is everywhere at the same time. God sees everything before it happens. When we are traveling, God sees the danger that we might face, and He will send us another way to avoid the danger. We as God's children always have the protection of God. Does this mean that we as God's children should be careless and never use wisdom? No, we must use our knowledge and wisdom of God in everything we do. We must always trust in God to fight every battle that comes our way. Scripture tells us that we as God's children must be mindful of God, and meditate on His word all day, and every day. This is the mindset that our Father wants us to have at all times. Why? Because, He is our life, and we are His children. God does not ever want His children to rely on their own strength but rather rely on Him for everything.

ASK HIM FOR WISDOM

"If any of you lacks wisdom, he should ask God who gives generously to all without finding fault, and it will be given to him."   ***James 1:5***

"The fear of the Lord is the beginning of wisdom; a good understanding have all those who do His commandments."   ***Psalm 111:10a***

There are two kinds of wisdoms, the world's wisdom, and God's wisdom. The wisdom of the world is foolishness to God. God catches men in all of their craftiness. The wisdom of God comes in the instructions you receive from God. When you have instructions from God, you have the power to do anything. It does not take worldly wisdom or intellect to accumulate anything in God's kingdom. It simply takes following His instructions. Yet, instructions from God seem foolish to many of the world. Sometimes instructions from God do not make sense to a child of God because His ways are so different from the ways of the world. This is why a child of God must always be seeking God and paying close attention to Him. God speaks in a very soft voice; and if a child of God has many distractions going on he could miss the instructions that God is giving him.

When a child of God asks God for wisdom, he must ask in faith and there must not be any doubting. If there are doubts, God will not give this person any wisdom. Understanding will also come to the child of God if he asks. In fact, God will give a child of His whatever he asks if it is in His will to do so.

In *2 Timothy 2:7,* it tells us that God will give us understanding. *"Consider what I say, and may the Lord give you understanding in all things."*

We as children of God must realize that all knowledge, wisdom and understanding are hidden in Jesus our Lord. When we abide in Him and He in us, we have access to these things. All we have to do is to ask and believe that He will give us what we ask.

It is said about the characteristic of wisdom, understanding and knowledge; wisdom builds the house, understanding establishes the house and knowledge decorates the house with the furnishings.

This is what the Bible says about the people of the world who consider themselves as being wise; *"Let no one deceive himself; if anyone among you seems to be wise in this age, let him become a fool that he may become wise. For the wisdom of this world is foolishness with God."* **1 Corinthians 3:18.**

Chapter Twenty-One
Pray About Everything

"Be anxious for nothing, but in everything by prayer and supplication with thanksgiving, let your request be known to God. And the peace that surpasses all understanding will guard your hearts and minds through Christ Jesus."

Philippians 4:6-7

"Therefore I say to you, whatever things you ask when you pray believing that you receive them, and you will have them." **Mark 11:24**

"The Lord is far from the wicked, but He hears the prayers of the righteous."

Psalm 15:29

PRAY ABOUT EVERYTHING

Pray about each and everything that we feel hopeless about, and all things we have no control over. We just need God to help us as soon as possible. Our needs and concerns maybe small or large, it does not matter to God. He has promised us that He is always available to hear our prayers. Scripture tells us that God always hear the prayers of a righteous person. Scripture teaches us that, *"The effective prayers of a righteous person avails much." **James 5:16b.***

God is our life and He is always concerned about the things that concern us. Just like our earthly parents are concerned about the things that concern us. We as the children of God are always on His mind and we should always have God on our mind because He is our life. It pleases God when we rely on Him for everything. We show our need for Him when we pray. If we do not pray, what message are we sending to God? Jesus said for us to bring the things to Him that are heavy laden to us. He is telling us to pray to Him about the things that are a burden to us and He will take them on Himself and He will bear them, and we will have peace and rest.

Scripture teaches us when we ask God for something that we want, do not just ask God one time and never ask Him again. We should ask Him again and again until we receive from Him what we are asking. His word tells us that He will give us what we ask of Him if we ask in faith and do not doubt. If we doubt that God will give us what we ask, we will not receive from Him what we are asking. Doubting will cancel our prayers every time. And we must remember that what we are asking God for must be in the will of God. If what we are asking God in prayer is not in His will, we will not receive what we are asking. We must believe that God will give us what we ask, even before we ask God. Scripture tells us that we must believe when we pray. In *Mark 11:24*, *"Therefore I say to you, whatever things you ask when you pray, believe that you receive them, and you will have them."* Believing God is one of the keys of receiving from God. And to believe Him we must first know God. If we do not know God, how can we believe Him? Scripture tells us that whoever comes to God must first believe Him. In *Hebrews 11:6*, it says, *"But without faith it is impossible to please Him, for he who comes to God must believe that He is, and He is a rewarder of those who diligently seek Him."* Seeking God is the only way to know Him. And it is a sure thing that when we seek Him with a pure heart He will reveal Himself to us. This is a promise of God to all His children.

HE GIVE US STRENGTH

"O God You are more awesome than Your holy places. The God of Israel is He who gives strength and power to His people."　　**Psalm 68:35**

"Do not be wise in your own eyes; fear the Lord and depart from evil, It will be health to your flesh, and strength to your bones."　　**Proverbs 3:7-8**

There are many benefits in being a child of God. One of those benefits is receiving strength from God when we need it. For God knows when His children are weak and weary and all we have to do is to ask Him for strength and He will give us strength. God made our bodies and He alone knows every function and how it works. To give His children strength is something that God desires to do for His children when they need strength. God made our bodies to withstand the toughest and the most gruesome adversities of life. Scripture tells us in **Psalm 139:14**, *"I will praise You, for I am fearfully and wonderfully made, marvelous are Your works, and that my soul knows very well."*

God is the ultimate owner of our bodies and He will keep our bodies according to His promises. By the stripes that Jesus received during crucifixion, we are healed from any ailments.

All we have to do is believe it and claim it and we will have our healing. This promise can be found in *Isaiah 53:5* For God knows everything that is good for our bodies and He has provided everything we need through His word. If we are obedient to the word of God He will see to it that we remain in excellent health. For God formed our inner parts. He covered us in our mother's womb. He did all these things in secret and our earthly parents had no knowledge that God was performing a miracle right before their eyes. We as God's children will always need Him in every way. And He made us to depend on Him for everything.

GOD PROMISE TO KEEP YOU SAFE

"We know that anyone born of God does not continue to sin; the one who was born of God keeps him safe, and the evil one cannot harm him. We know that we are children of God, and that the world is under the control of the evil one."

1 John 5:18

Remember it is God who desires to give you all of His promises, but not until He has trained and changed you from the world's way of living. The promises of God are only for His children and not for the world. The children of the world have rejected the knowledge of Jesus Christ and they do not know God and the power of His word. God loves all people and He has made a way for those who love Him. For God hears the cries of those who do not have food in the world. The Bible tells me that God sympathies and He saves. His heart goes out to those who are poor and without food. God's children must act as His representative on earth, assisting those who cannot help themselves. God gives His children an assignment to do His will. For God gives special blessings to those who considers the poor. In the book of **Psalm 41:1,** it tells us, *"Blessed is he who considers the poor; The Lord will deliver him in time of trouble. The Lord will preserve him, and keep him alive; and he shall be blessed upon the earth; And I will not deliver him to his enemies. The Lord will strengthen him upon his bed of illness; The Lord will sustain him on his sickbed."*

We as God's children must not forget the poor. If we do not have the funds to send to the poor, we can always pray for the poor. For this is pleasing to God. This shows that we care for them and love them. These are promises (and benefits) that God has made available to those who love and consider the poor: blessings, deliverance, protection from trouble, preservation, prosperity, and restoration of health when sick. We must remember that Jesus fed the poor when He was on earth. Therefore, we as the children of God must do the same

Speak To Your Circumstances

Jesus was our example when He walked on the earth. He did many miracles and He helped those who had needs. He taught His disciples to do the same thing that He did. He taught His disciples that they could speak to their problems if they could only believe and not doubt. Jesus was walking and He observed that the fig tree only had leaves, no fruit. He commanded that the tree would not produce any fruit again. The fig tree withered and died. Jesus told His disciples if they believed and did not doubt they could say to the mountain be removed and be cast into the sea. It would obey them. Jesus was not talking about a physical mountain, He was talking about problems in their lives. Jesus was teaching His disciples to imitate what He was doing. But they must believe that they could do what He was doing. Remember God wanted children on the earth. And He gave His children some of His own attributes and some of His powers through His Son Jesus. Jesus was saying that if we have the faith and believe, we could also do the things that he did.

God wants He children to speak to their circumstances and get the same results that Jesus got when He spoke to the fig tree.

It is the power of God's word that is in operation when we speak to our circumstances. It is about our belief and our relationship with God that will cause us to speak to our circumstances and get results. We are to imitate God as the word of God tells us to in **Ephesians 5:1** *"Therefore be imitators of God as dear children."*

When we obey God and speak to our circumstances, we must speak with authority and belief. We should never doubt the word of God. The

128

word of God has supreme power over everything on earth. Jesus is in every committed child of God. His power exists on the inside of us also. The Bible tells us that what is on the inside of us is greater than what is in this world. **One John 4:4** says, *"You are of God, little children, and have overcome them, because He that is in you is greater than he who is in the world."* It is good to know that when we are in Jesus and He is in us we have overcome the world. We can always put the devil in his place.

When God gave us, the life of Jesus, to dwell inside of us, He also gave us power to do great things through Him.

Chapter Twenty-Two

God Wants To Provide For You

"And my God shall supply all my needs according to His riches in Glory by Christ Jesus" **Philippians 4:19**

"He who did not spare His own Son, but delivered Him up for us all; How shall He not with Him, freely give us all things." **Romans 8:32**

HIS GIFT OF SALVATION

The greatest gift God could ever bestow upon anyone is the gift of salvation. The gift is so great that no money in the world could pay for salvation. For salvation is priceless and the only way salvation could be purchased is through the blood of a person who had never sinned and that is Jesus Christ the Son of God. He paid our sin debt in full with His own life. Because of the love of God, we have eternal life and we are free to approach the throne of God at any time because of what Jesus did on the cross. The Scripture teaches us, *"For through Him, we both have access by one Spirit to the Father."* **Ephesians 2:18**

We have Jesus who is our great High Priest who has passed through the heavens, Jesus the Son of God. Let us hold fast to our confession. Because He is our great High Priest, Scripture tells us in **Hebrews 4:16,** *"Let us therefore come boldly to the throne of grace, that we may obtain mercy and find grace to help in time of need."* We as God's children can approach the throne of God at any time and seek Him for grace and mercy.

Under the old law, only the high priest could approach God in the Holy of Holies and the high priest went before God on behalf of the people. This teaching is explained in Hebrews. Under the terms of the old covenant, the Jewish people did not have access to the Holy of Holies, the dwelling place of the Lord's presence. Only the high priest could enter it, but not without a blood sacrifice. Only once a year was He allowed to cover his sins and the sins of the people. Jesus died on the cross as the ultimate offering for sin, making the way for us to have a personal relationship with God. Today He is our High Priest and it is no longer necessary to have an earthly priest to partition God for us.

Just think about what Jesus did for us on the cross. He made it possible to do what only the priest could do under the old covenant. He could only go before the presence of God once a year. Jesus made it possible for us to go before God as many times as necessary; and we do not have to take blood to do it. God will hear His children as often as they pray to Him. This is the love that He has for His children. Jesus paid this price for us to approach God. The hope is that the children of God can appreciate the benefit of the privilege made possible by Jesus Christ.

Why did God choose salvation for us? The answer is simple: God wants all of His children to be close to him because He is our heavenly Father. First and foremost, He loves us and only wants the best for us. He has already conveyed this to us through the love, hopes, and dreams our parents have for us. When He is ready and believes we are ready, He will call on us directly. Hopefully, you will recognize His call. I did:

In the fall of 1982, I quickly accepted His Son as my Lord and Savior after an encounter in a restaurant in Atlanta, Georgia.

I was sitting in a restaurant having a meal when a person at a neighboring table asked to join me. I replied yes. He began to talk about the Bible and I asked some questions about the Bible that I did not understand. I listened as he answered my questions. I had planned to meet a friend later that evening, but I became so involved in our discussion that I completely forgot about my nine o'clock meeting with my friend. Four hours later, we were still talking about the things of the Bible.

We parted around eleven o'clock and I went home. I opened my Bible and began to read the Scriptures. Although I had read the Bible on several occasions, but this time it was quite different. I seemed to have had an understanding like never before. It was as if the words I read emanated from the Spirit of God. At first, it was a little scary. I knew something was happening to me but I could not quite explain it.

The next day I gave my life to Jesus and accepted Him in my life. From that point on, I made a conscious commitment to know God. I began to study the Scripture diligently to learn the truth and to get to know God.

After five or six months, God revealed Himself to me. I will never forget it! I kept thinking to myself, God showed Himself to me. I kept repeating this over, and over in my head. I did not know how to explain it to anyone so I kept it to myself and continued seeking to know Him better.

October 20, 2007, God called me into the ministry. I remember it like it was yesterday. It was about nine o'clock in the evening when I received a phone call from a person that I did not know. To this day, I know that God arranged that phone call and spoke to me through the caller, who later began to mentor me on the secret things of God.

The Scripture teaches us *this* truth in **John 15:16,** *"You did not choose Me, but I chose you and appointed you that you should go and bear fruit, and that your fruit should remain, that whatever you ask the Father in My name He may give to you."*

Now I understand I was saved through His grace, and not through anything I did. I was a lost person who did not know God. He drew me close to Him, and I responded by accepting His calling. ***Ephesians 2:8*** tells us, *"For by grace you have been saved through faith, and not of yourselves;*

it is a gift of God not of works, lest anyone should boast."

GOD PROMISES TO GIVE US GOOD THINGS

"If you then being evil know how to give good gifts to your children, how much more will your Father who is in heaven know how to give good things to those who ask Him."   ***Matthew 7:11***

All people love to receive gifts and parents love to give gifts to their children. It is a natural thing to want to give to your children. God knows that His children love good gifts and He wants to give them good things. He wants His children to have the best in life. He wanted the Israelite children to have the best land and the best environment possible. God made plans to place them in the promise land known as the land of milk and honey. However, God wanted to change them before they entered the new land. God kept the Israelites in the wilderness for forty years refining and attempting to change their character. Later, this would prove not to be what they wanted. They refused to change and they became rebellious and disobedient. God decided that the entire first generation of Israelites except for Joshua and Caleb would not enter in the promise land. They perished in the wilderness because they chose not to change.

Throughout Scripture, it tells us repeatedly that God wants the best for His children. God will always prepare His children before He rewards them with His best. Scripture tells us that God will train every child that comes to Him. ***Hebrews 12:6*** tell us, *"For whom the Lord loves, He chastens and scourges every son whom He receives."*

We must remember that God gave us His best when He gave us His Son Jesus Christ. Therefore, if He gave us His Son what else will He give us? Better said, what will He not give us? I believe that children of God have so much to look forward to in their upcoming life with Jesus. God owns everything and we are heirs of God. This means that we own everything also. Scripture teaches us in **Romans 8:16-17,** *"The Spirit Himself bears witness with our spirit that we are the children of God, and if children, then heirs of God and joint heirs with Christ, if indeed we suffer with Him, that we may also be glorified with Him together."*

This suggests that the children of God, as heirs of God, can expect to be glorified with Jesus, This is His will and our hope. God has it all planned and prepared for all who love Him and obey His commands. I have always believed that God is a God of all great things in life. I have observed what He has done down through history for those who loved Him and obeyed Him. I focused on what He gave to Adam and Eve and how He wanted to be a provider for their every need.

I read what He did for Joseph and how He kept His promise to him. Joseph became governor of Egypt and a blessing to his own family. God also provided so much to Abraham and Sarah. God made King Abimelech of Gerar give Abraham one thousand pieces of silver, sheep, oxen and servants to take with him. The King gave these gifts to Abraham because he feared God for keeping Abraham's wife in his palace.

God wants to give great things to His children who obey Him and live a life that is pleasing to Him. God's children can ask Him for great things. It is our faith and belief in God that ultimately allow us to receive what He has promised. This is what the word of God says in

Ephesians 3:20, *"Now to Him who is able to do exceedingly abundantly above all that we ask or think, according to the power that works in us."*

We must always remember that the things that we ask of God must be in His will. If the things that we ask are not in the will of God, He will not give us these things, nor will He hear our prayers for these things. I believe that God will give to His children as much as their faith will allow.

The Bible tells me that God wants His children to have joy, peace and happiness and He wants His children to have everlasting wealth. Those who do not please God will not keep the wealth they have according to the word of God. God will allow them to gather and collect wealth in order to hand it over to the children who are pleasing to God. This teaching is in *Ecclesiastes 2:26.*

LIVE A LIFE THAT IS PLEASING TO GOD...

Chapter Twenty-Three

We Are The Righteousness Of God

"For he made Him who knew no sin to be sin for us, that we might become the righteousness of God in Him."   **2 Corinthians 5:21**

"In the way of righteousness is life, and in the pathway there is no death."

Proverbs 12:28

We Are The Righteousness Of God

Scripture tells us that we are to seek the kingdom of God and His righteousness, and all things will be added unto us. There is only righteousness and justice in the kingdom of God. It is the will of God that all of His children enter His kingdom. None of the children of God will perish in His kingdom. If you are a child of God, you can only be in the wilderness or in the kingdom of God. If you are in the kingdom of God, you have already been in the wilderness. If you are in the wilderness, you are heading to the kingdom of God. The wilderness is the place where God trains and changes us to produce fruit. He does not want us to stay in the wilderness. He wants us to change so that we will eventually enter His kingdom and His rest. For this is the ultimate place God wants all His children to be and that is in His rest.

We as the children of God are the righteousness of God. We are His ambassadors and representatives in Christ Jesus. We are a beacon light to the unsaved and the lost. When a lost person sees you, they should see a glimpse of the character of Jesus Christ. Some people never read the Bible and upon seeing you, they may experience the closest encounter they will ever have with the Spirit of God.

Scripture tells us that God loves righteousness and His children are the righteousness of God through Jesus. This is one of the reasons that God wants His children to bear much fruit. The fruit that He wants us to produce is the fruit of the Spirit, which is love, joy, kindness, gentleness, peace, longsuffering, faithfulness, self-control and goodness.

We were made in the image of God. Thus, we should love the things He loves and hate the things He hates. The devil and his angels are busy operating in the things that God hates. The devil is promoting unrighteousness and injustice. The devil is the author of all lies and he is not about truth. The Bible tells us that he has deceived the whole world. Exiled from heaven, the devil and his angels sent to reside on earth. The devil's mission is to kill, steal and destroy as many people on earth as it is possible. God has already made a place in hell for the devil and his angels. The devil wants to take as many people with him to his final resting place and that is hell.

DON'T LIVE ON BREAD ALONE

Jesus said to him, *"It is written, man shall not live by bread alone, but by every word that proceeds from the mouth of God."* **Matthew 4:4**

The Bible clearly tells us that we cannot live by bread alone. We have to include the word of God in our diet. If we do not include the word of God in our dict, we will surely die according to the teaching of Jesus Christ. If a person does not live by the word of God, he will surely perish from this life. In **Hosea 4:6,** it tells us, *"My people are destroyed for the lack of knowledge."* There are people who do not want to know the word of God and therefore they have rejected the word of God by choice. God says, "Because you have rejected knowledge, I also will reject you as being my priest, and since you have forgotten the law of your God, I also will forget your children."

God has made it clear to us that we cannot live the life that He wants us to live without His word. There are many people who are trying to do just that. I was one of those persons many years ago when I did not know God and did not have a personal relationship with Him. I was living a perishing lifestyle and did not know it. By the mercy of God, He drew me to Himself and I was saved by His grace through Jesus Christ. Now I am producing fruit in my life, so that others can see the light in me and be induced to follow Christ. To live on bread alone is to try to live on anything that money can buy. To try to live on anything that money can buy without the word of God will lead to a perishing lifestyle.

We live in a society today that sends a message that material things are necessary to live. Too many people buy into this mindset and believe there are certain material things they must have to exist. The world does not advocate the need of God or His word. The world thinks the things of God are foolishness and therefore, they have their own gods and their idols. Anything that we place before God is an idol. This could be sports, entertainment, church, other people, our spouse or mate, etc.

Scripture teaches us that no one can live without the word of God. For God did not make man to live without Him. Man can exist without God for a while, but it is almost as if he is challenging God to prove Him wrong. However, God will not be mocked; whatever a man sows, he will reap. Whenever a person plants a seed of unbelief and he lives as if there is no God, these seeds of unbelief will come up in time and visit upon this person. God created this earth in a way that there will always be seed time and harvest. Whatever we plant will come up as a harvest in its time. Scripture tells us in *Genesis 8:22, "As long as the earth remains seedtime and harvest, and cold and heat, and summer and winter, and day and night, shall not cease."*

Program Your Mind With The Word Of God

"My son, give attention to My words, incline your ear to my saying, Do not let them depart from your eyes; keep them in the midst of your heart, for they are life to those who find them, and health to all their flesh." **Proverb 4:22**

Jesus has told us that the word of God is life to those who believe. We as the children of God should choose life and not cursing. When we do not choose life, we are choosing cursing. When we choose to embrace God's word and live it daily in Jesus, Scripture tells me that we will receive blessings from God. Our children will be blessed also because of our obedience to God by choosing life. **Deuteronomy 30:19** There is no greater habit than the habit of reading and studying the word of God. As you absorb the word of God into your spirit, you are inputting life in your body. There will be healing to your body and strength to your bones according to Scripture. For this is a promise of God to all of His children. In time as the child of God continues to read, study and meditate on the word of God, he will begin to demonstrate the love of God in his life. He is planting the word of God in his heart, and whatever is planted in the heart of man will come out of the mouth of man. When a person takes in his heart the word of God with the intent to know God, he is planting the best seed possible to be what God has called him to be.

God has called His children to Him to produce much fruit; the kind of fruit that will last forever. When a child of God is producing fruit, God can use him for the work of His kingdom. The fruit I am referring to is love, peace, joy, kindness, goodness, gentleness, longsuffering, patience and self-control. God wants this character in His children.

God can place the desire of the fruit of the Spirit in the hearts of all of His children. Other words, in time we will desire the things that God desires for us. We will want to love others and be kind to them. We will be patient with others and be considerate of their short- comings. We will be willing to trust God and wait on Him for our request, rather than be anxious for God to act when we want Him to act. It all comes down to a child of God being willing to wait on God. And what will be the deciding factor that will ultimately cause a child of God to wait on Him, the love for God that is in the heart of the child of God.

SEEKING GOD'S PLAN FOR YOUR LIFE

The Scripture tells us that God has a plan for all of His children and He wants His children to know what plans He has for them. However, God wants His children to seek Him for the plan He has for them. Just how does a child of God seek Him to know this plan? In *Jeremiah 29:11* it says, *"I know the plan I have for you, "declares the lord, plans to prosper you and not harm you, plans to give you hope and a future."* Now we know that God said that He has a plan for us, it is time to get to know Him and ask Him for the plan for our life.

We must seek Him with everything that is in us and he will hear our prayer and give us the plan for our life. The Bible tells us to do this. *"Then you will call upon Me and come and pray to Me, and I will listen to you. You will seek Me and find Me when you seek Me with all of your heart".* *Jeremiah 29:12-13,* You will find God only when you seek Him with all of your heart. After you find Him, ask Him to reveal to you the plan He has for you. You must continue to ask Him again, and again until

He gives it to you. If you really want God's plan, you must ask more than one time. If you only ask Him one time and forget it, He may forget also.

God will train and prepare you for the plan He has for you. He will begin His training with you by teaching you His ways, which are different from the ways of the world to which you are accustomed. God will proceed the training by removing everything from you that you have learned from the world. This process will require discipline from God who loves as a Father should love a son. In *Hebrews 12:5b,* *"My son, do not make light of the Lord's discipline, and do not lose heart when He rebukes you, because the Lord disciplines those He loves, and He punishes everyone He accepts as a son."* No discipline seems pleasant at the time, but painful. Later on however, it produces a harvest of righteousness and peace for those who have been trained by it. *Hebrews 12:11*

How can you do the assignment that God has planned for you without God training you? It is impossible. No one can do the assignment that God has for him without the training from God Himself. Many people who have been given assignments by God, but they have not yet allowed God to train them. They cannot be successful doing the things of God without the proper training of God. They are completely on an assignment of their own and in their own strength. How can God be in the person's assignment, if they did not wait on God to lead them? God is not pleased with anyone who does not wait on His direction to lead them with the plan He has for them. To the man who is pleasing to God He gives wisdom, knowledge and happiness, but to the sinner He gives the task of gathering and storing up wealth to hand it over to the one who pleases God. *Ecclesiastes 2:26.*

Chapter Twenty-Four
God's Servants Who Displeased Him

"Fear God and keep His commandments, for this is the whole duty of man. For God will bring every deed into judgment, including every hidden thing, whether it is good or evil." **Ecclesiastes 12:13-14**

Just because God chooses you to perform an assignment for Him and you obeyed Him, this does not mean you are exempt from being obedient at any time in the future.

The characters outlined in this chapter were indeed chosen by God to carry out the will of God in a particular service. And all of them at one time or another decided that they would disobey God. When we as children of God make a decision to disobey God, often times He will forgive us. However, the act of disobedience has its consequences. God will decide on what the consequences will be.

WHEN ADAM AND EVE DISPLEASED GOD

God placed Adam and Eve in The Garden of Eden and provided everything they needed to live. He gave instructions on what fruit trees to eat from and what trees not to eat. There was one tree God told them not to eat. He told them if they ate from this tree, they would surely die. The devil came to Eve as she was near the forbidden tree and he questioned her about what God had said. She told the devil that if they ate from this one tree of good and evil that they would die. The serpent (devil) said to Eve, *"You will not surely die.' For God knows that when you eat of it your eyes will be opened, and you will be like God, knowing good from evil." **Genesis 3:4-5***

When Eve saw that the fruit of the tree was good for food and pleasing to the eye, and also desirable for gaining wisdom, she took some and ate it. She also gave some to her husband, who was with her, and he ate it. The eyes of both of them were opened, and they realized they were naked; so they sewed fig leaves together and made coverings for themselves. God banished Adam and Eve from the Garden of Eden forever, because He did not want them to have access to the tree of life ever again. *Genesis 3:16*

The consequence: God greatly increased the pain for women during childbirth.

WHEN CAIN DISPLEASED GOD

Adam and Eve had two sons, Cain and Abel. Cain tended the land and Abel had cattle. In time, the two brothers brought an offering to God. God had given instructions to both of them on how to present their offers. The instructions were to be the first and the best of their harvest. Cain presented his offering to God, which was from the fruit of the ground. Abel also brought his offer to God, which was the first and best of his harvest. The Lord respected Abel's offering, but He did not respect Cain's offering. Cain's offering was not of his first or best of the land.

Because God disrespected Cain's offering, he became angry and indignant. Cain talked his brother Abel into going with him into the field. Cain killed his brother Abel. God cursed Cain and told him that he would be a restless wanderer on the earth. *Genesis 4:8*

The consequence: Cain became a restless wanderer on earth for the rest of his life. Furthermore, the blood of his brother Abel would be on his hand for the rest of his life. He would be a fugitive with a murderous consciousness forever. Could there ever be any peace for his soul?

WHEN KING DAVID DISPLEASED GOD

King Saul was the king of Israel and after his death, David succeeded him as king of Israel. One day as King David was walking on the roof of his palace he saw a woman bathing. She was a beautiful woman and David sent one of his officials to bring her to him. David took the woman and laid with her and later he discovered that she was the wife of one the men in David's army. Her name was Bathsheba and her husband was Uriah a devoted man of David's army. Later, Bathsheba told kind David that she was going to have a child. David sent one of his servants whose name was Joab to have Uriah to report to the king. Uriah came to David and the king sent Uriah home to be with his wife. However, Uriah went to the room for the palace guard and slept there that night and he did not go home. The next day King David discovered that Uriah did not go home so King David invited Uriah for dinner. King David gave Uriah drinks to make him drunk and afterwards he ordered Uriah to go home to his wife, but he did not go home. David sent a letter to the army commander by Joab to have Uriah placed at the front of the battlefield and have everyone else to retreat and leave Uriah in a risky position to be killed. He was killed when King David's army drew back and left him to fend for himself before the enemies. After the death of Uriah, David took Bathsheba for his wife. God was displeased with David when Bathsheba gave birth to a son. God did not allow the child to live and David was sad and prayed to God for forgiveness. God forgave David, but God will not allow the child to live. David lamented before his servants. God developed an adversity against King David, took his wives, and gave them to those who were close to him. God told David that what you did in secret, I will do this

150

in broad daylight before Israel. *2 Samuel 12:7*

The consequence: David's son by Bathsheba died. God took all of David's wives and gave them to those who were close to him.

WHEN KING SOLOMON DISPLEASED GOD

Solomon, the son of King David built a temple of God that God would not allow King David to build. David had the blood of Uriah, the husband of Bathsheba on his hand, so God refused to let him build the temple. God blessed King Solomon with wisdom that no one had seen in that time. As King Solomon grew older, his wives talked him into worshipping other gods and wooden idols. Solomon's father David was always devoted to the Lord and never became an idolater. King David talked to his son about serving the Lord and keeping His commandments. His wives turned him away from the Lord Almighty and He became disobedient to the point of serving the same false gods of his wives. He even built shrines on the hill east of Jerusalem to worship Chemosh the disgusting god of Ammon. By this time, King Solomon had become a full-fledged Idolater. God hated idol worshipping and He would not tolerate the practice of it. King Solomon had fallen to his lowest point. The Lord appeared to Solomon twice to warn him not to worship other gods, but Solomon disobeyed God and continued to worship other gods. This made the Lord very angry so God punished Solomon by taking his kingdom. He gave it to the men of Solomon's offices. God told Solomon that He would allow him to remain king as long as he lived but when Solomon's son became King, God would take the kingdom away from his son. The wrath of God fell on Solomon's son Rehoboam. God took the kingdom away from Rehoboam before his kingship ended. *2 Chronicles 12:1*

The consequence: God ceased the kingship of Solomon's family while Solomon's son was king.

WHEN MOSES DISPLEASED GOD

God commissioned Moses to go to Egypt and confront Pharaoh the ruler of Egypt to free the Israelite people. According to Scripture, these people had been in slave bondage for over four hundred years. After Pharaoh released the Israelites, God did not allow Moses to march them right into the promise land. God had to change the Israelites slave ways to His ways. All the Israelites knew was slavery and God's intention was to train them to walk in His ways. This was more easy said than done, for the Israelites refused to change their ways. They constantly complained to Moses about the food God gave them. They wanted meat in their daily diet and not just the manna that God provided for them every day. God provided the manna daily and He provided water. One time during their travel, they did not have water and Moses went before God and asked God to provide water. Then the Lord spoke to Moses saying, *"take the rod; you and your brother Aaron gather the people together. Speak to the rock before their eyes, and it will yield its water; thus you shall bring water for them out of the rock, and give drink to the people and their animals."* **Numbers 20:8.** Therefore, Moses and Aaron gathered the people before the rock and he said to them, *"Hear now you* *rebels! Must we bring water to you out of this rock?" v:10* Then Moses lifted his hand and struck the rock twice with his rod; and water came out abundantly, so the people and their animals drank. The people were happy because they had water to drink, but God was not pleased with Moses because he did not obey Him. God told Moses to speak to the rock, not strike the rock for water. Then the Lord spoke to Moses and Aaron; *"Because you did not believe Me, to hallow Me in the eyes of the children of Israel, therefore you shall not bring this people into the promise land which I have given them." v: 12*

The consequences: God did not allow Moses to lead the Israelites into the promise land.

WHEN KING SAUL DISPLEASED GOD

In a city of Ephraim, there was a woman named Hannah who did not have children and she prayed to God to give her a son. She told God that if He would give her a son, she would give him to the Lord and God answered her prayers.

In the course of time, Hannah conceived and she gave birth to a son. She named him Samuel and she kept her word and presented the boy before the Lord to a prophet named Eli.

Eli mentored the child in the ways of the Lord, and he grew up in the presence of the Lord. The boy Samuel ministered before the Lord under Eli. One night as Samuel was laying down on his bed; the Lord appeared to him and said, *"Samuel, Samuel!' Then Samuel said 'Speak, for*

your servant is listening.' And the Lord said: 'See, I am about to do something in Israel that will make the ears of everyone who hears of it tingle. At that time, I will carry out against Eli everything against his family from beginning to end."
1 Samuel 3:10-12

For God had warned Eli about the behavior of his sons. Eli had not constrained his sons from immoral acts in the temple with women. God was not pleased with how Eli governed the behavior of his sons.

Samuel is later recognized as a prophet of God since the Lord appeared to him through His word. Saul later became the King of Israel, mainly because he was a foot taller than anyone in Israel. During a battle between Israel and the Philistines, Samuel had received instructions from the Lord to have Saul to wait seven days until his return. When Samuel returned Saul had already ordered his servant to bring animals to him to sacrifice to God. Only a prophet had the authority to make an offering. Saul made an offering to God for victory over the Philistine army. Samuel told Saul that it was a stupid thing for him to do. Saul said that he had to force himself to make an offering to God to ask for help. Samuel told Saul that he had disobeyed God by not waiting on him. *1 Samuel 13:8*

The consequence: God would not allow anyone from Saul's family to continue the kingship after Saul.

WHEN AARON DISPLEASED GOD

While the Israelites were camped at the foot of Mount Sinai, God called Moses up on the mountain to give him the tablets of the Ten Commandments. God kept Moses on the mountain for forty days and the Israelite people begin to complain. They said to Aaron that God had brought them out in the wilderness to die. They did not want to wait on Moses any longer. Moses left his Brother Aaron in charge of the leadership of the entire congregation. The people rebelled against Aaron and demanded that he build them an idol of a golden calf. Aaron agreed and asked everyone to bring him all of the gold in their possession. Aaron built an idol of gold for the people to worship and they had an idol party. God saw what was going on in the camp and was angry at the Israelites. God told Moses to return to the camp because the people had committed a great sin. They had become foolish and rebellious. Moses asked God to forgive the sins of the people and God said, "Whoever has sinned against Me I will blot out of My book." Moses returned to the camp and saw the people rivaling and worshipping the golden calf. Moses became angry at the Israelites and he threw the two tablets of the Ten Commandments at the people and broke both tablets. Later God called Moses back to the mountain to get two new tablets to replace the first two broken tablets. *Exodus 32:1-24*

The consequence: Aaron did not enter the Promise Land of the first generation Israelites, only Joshua and Caleb entered the promise land. And of the second generation all twenty year olds and younger entered the promise land.

155

WHEN JONAH DISPLEASED GOD

God sent Jonah to a city of Nineveh, which was the capital of Assyrian. God wanted Jonah to preach the gospel to the people of this city and have them to repent of their sins. But Jonah decided that he would not have anything to do with the people of Nineveh. So he went to Joppa to board a ship that was headed to Tarshish. He disobeyed God and went to Tarshish instead of Nineveh. While he was on the ship, God sent a strong wind against the ship that was so strong it was about to break the ship apart. The captain told everyone abroad to pray to his god for safety and the crew did just that. However, the wind did not cease its fury. Jonah told the ship crew that if they threw him over board they would all live because he was the problem. The men threw Jonah off the ship and God caused a large fish to swallow Jonah. Jonah remained in the belly of the fish for three days and three nights. God commanded the large fish to spit Jonah up on the shore exactly where he had first boarded the ship in Joppa. Jonah proceeded to the city of Nineveh where God had commanded him to go before he boarded the ship in Joppa.

Jonah preached in the city of Nineveh and the entire city believed his message and received God. *Jonah 2:10*

The consequence: Jonah was swallowed by a large fish. He remained in the belly of the fish three days and three nights.

Conclusion

A life that is pleasing to God is a life that can only be lived through Jesus Christ the Son of God. There is no other way that is pleasing to Him. God wants His children to Abide in Jesus always and allow the word of God to abide in us. This is the only way we can live a successful life. This is the life that God tells His children to live, in order to receive His blessings. If we choose to live any other way, than by Jesus there will not be any blessings from God.

Jesus is the believer's life and only hope. God has given Him authority in both heaven and earth. Jesus sent the Holy Spirit into the lives of all of God's children as our helper and Comforter to help in time of need. The Holy Spirit also helps us in living a life that is pleasing to God. Without the Holy Spirit to show us the way, it would be impossible to follow the teaching of Jesus Christ. It is not difficult to live a Spiritual life with the help of the Holy Spirit. For God gave us everything we need to bear fruit in this life.

The Bible tells us that the whole duty of man is to fear Him and obey His commands. When we fear Him, it is the beginning of wisdom. Surely, wisdom is the principle thing. Therefore, we should get wisdom. God proved His love for all of us by sending His Son to give His life for us, so that we could have eternal life and be with Him forever. God also wants His children to have the best that this life can offer. He wanted the best for the Israelites and their families, so He freed them from bondage of Egyptian slavery and gave them the promise land. Today God wants to give his children His very best. His very best is contained in the promises that He has already made to us. Scripture tells us in **Romans 8:32(NIV),** *"He who did not spare His own Son, but gave him up for us all—how will he not also, along with him, graciously give us all things."* Just think how much love God had for us that He gave His only Son that we may have life after death that will never end. The Bible also teaches us that God is managing the life and the circumstances of all His children. We are not living a life of risk like the unsaved people of the earth. We are not subject to the troubles of life like those who do not serve God. Because we serve and obey God, we are living a life fully protected by Him.

The fully committed children of God can rely on God for everything He said He would do. Not one word has ever failed of the precious promises that God gave us. We can always depend on God's word and His promises. However, we must live a life that is pleasing to God to receive His promises. Therefore, before we receive His promises He will train us according to His word in **Hebrews 12:11.** After the training God puts us through, He will prepare His children for His promises.

About The Author

Odell Young Jr. has authored three scriptural books: *Only God Can Give You the Power to Get Wealth*, *God's Promises for Every Believer to Live By*, and *Live a Life that is Pleasing to God*. God called Odell to be an ambassador of Jesus Christ on October 20, 2007. Since then, his life has centered on teaching the knowledge of the promises of God. He received his training, by way of the Holy Spirit, from Michael Coley, an apostle of God. Odell has been in training for over 6 years, since the conception of his first book.

Odell is a graduate of Morehouse College in Atlanta Georgia. He and his wife Delores live in Palmetto Georgia. They were blessed with three children, Angela, DeAnn, and Kevin.

In the fall of October 2007, God revealed to Odell that he had been doing business the world's way rather than God's way. His first spiritual book, Only God Can Give You the Power to Get Wealth, is the outcome of his relationship with God, and spiritual journey into new business ventures— doing God's work and getting wealth God's way. This book is a "how to" guide for you, a believer, to become empowered to gain wealth. Odell explains, "It is God who gives the believer the power to get wealth. When God gives you wealth, He adds no trouble to it."

ISBN-10: 0615311586
ISBN-13: 978-0615-31158-6
$19.95 USA

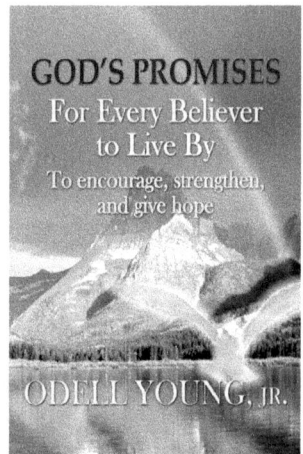

God's Promises For Every Believer to Live By explores the promises that God has made to His people throughout the world. These promises are available to every believer that seeks Him with all his heart. Young demonstrates how to prepare oneself to receive God's promises. Young explains "preparation comes through a commitment and dedication to studying His word, and the development of an intimate and daily relationship with Him." Uncover "step-by-step," the knowledge of how to live the life God intended for you when you receive His promises.

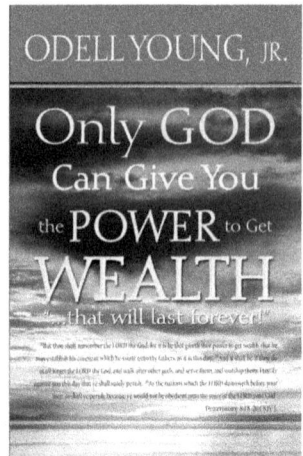

ISBN-10: 0615645100
ISBN-13: 978-0615645100
$17.00 USA